Gullah Home Cooking *the* Daufuskie Way

Gullah Home Cooking the Daufuskie Way

Smokin' Joe Butter Beans, Ol' 'Fuskie Fried Crab Rice, Sticky-Bush Blackberry Dumpling, & Other Sea Island Favorites

SALLIE ANN ROBINSON

with GREGORY WRENN SMITH

Foreword by PAT CONROY

The University of North Carolina Press

Chapel Hill and London

Set in Adobe Caslon and Rosewood by Eric M. Brooks
Manufactured in the United States of America
The paper in this book meets the guidelines for permanence and durability of the Committee on Production Guidelines for Book Longevity of the Council on Library Resources.

Library of Congress Cataloging-in-Publication Data
Robinson, Sallie Ann.
Gullah home cooking the Daufuskie way: smokin' joe butter beans, ol' 'fuskie fried crab rice, sticky-bush blackberry dumpling, and other Sea Island favorites / by Sallie Ann Robinson, with Gregory Wrenn Smith.
p. cm.
Includes index.
ISBN 0-8078-2783-5 (cloth: alk. paper)
ISBN 0-8078-5456-5 (pbk.: alk. paper)
1. Cookery, American—Southern style. 2. Gullah cookery—South Carolina. I. Smith, Gregory Wrenn. II. Title.
TX715.2.S68 R65 2003
641.59757—dc21 2002015048

cloth 07 06 05 04 03 5 4 3 2 1
paper 07 06 05 04 03 5 4 3 2 1

FOR POP & MOMMA

Life is a precious gift. Parents give it to you.

CONTENTS

FOREWORD

In 1969, I found myself twenty-three years old steering a boat across the May River in Bluffton, navigating a tricky route to a mysterious place called Daufuskie Island. It was the first year of "teacher integration" in the public school system in South Carolina, and I spent one of the richest and most pleasurable years of my life teaching eighteen black children from grades 5 through 8 in a two-room schoolhouse in the middle of a Carolina sea island that did not have a single paved road.

Until that time, segregation had been the law of the land in the South, and I was raised up in a tradition of a "separate but equal" school system. It took me a single morning with my new students to discover the equal part was a complete lie. My eighteen students all read below the first-grade level, five could not write their names or complete the ABC's, and none of them knew the name of the ocean that washed against the eastern shore of their pristine and paradisiacal island. They lived in one of the most beautiful and undiscovered places on earth, and all of those Daufuskie children had the run of the island.

That night I wrote the superintendent of schools a fiery, intemperate letter denouncing the school system for its cruel incompetence. The superintendent did not like my letter, did not like me, and twelve months later fired me for gross neglect of duty, conduct unbecoming a professional educator, being AWOL, and insubordination. Though he stole my teaching career from me, he could not touch that magnificent, life-changing year the children of Daufuskie had handed me like a gift.

I leapt into the kids' lives and they caught me with their arms wide open. They'd never heard of Halloween, and I took them to my hometown for Halloween. They'd never heard of Washington, D.C., and I took them to spend five days in one of my favorite cities in the world. Though they had never heard of classical music, when the deputy school superintendent came out for his annual visit, I encouraged several of the kids to get into a heated discussion, arguing whether they preferred Beethoven, Tschaikovsky, or Rimsky-Korsakov. One of those kids was the impish and delightful Sallie Ann Robinson, the author of this splendid book.

When I heard that Sallie Ann, a child of Daufuskie, was publishing a book with the University of North Carolina Press, it ranked with the best days of my life. I know the full measure of struggle that she endured in her quest to lift herself out of a life of great hardship to be published by an arm of the university that gave Thomas Wolfe to the world. I know the names of many of the people and the teachers who came after me. I know about "the California boys and girls" from the University of California, Santa Cruz, and the great, charismatic Herman Blake, who provided a free education for some of the Daufuskie kids. That Sallie Ann Robinson is the author of a published book is a bright miracle that adds grandeur and hope to the American story we are all telling.

Here is the great glory of this book, though—it will teach you how to eat much better than you did before you read it. My year on Daufuskie was one of the best-fed years of my overfed life. Daufuskie Islanders make the best deviled crab and deviled eggs—they are terrific with all dishes with the word "devil" in them. Sallie Ann could make biscuits that were light and feathery and teacher-pleasing when she was eleven years old. The island teems with deer and boar, rabbit and quail. The waters around it are tide-swollen, bringing the billion-footed incursion of shrimp into the rivers and marshes where Daufuskie nets await them for transportation to the kitchen tables of the island. I ate like a king in my one year on the island, and you will eat like me because Sallie Ann Robinson, one of the children I loved and taught, and wrote about in *The Water Is Wide*, grew up and got herself smart and ambitious and wonderful—and decided to write herself a book. I think I may be the proudest man on earth.

Pat Conroy

ACKNOWLEDGMENTS

It all begins with Pop and Momma. As far back as I can remember, I have happy memories of the old days, now long gone but never forgotten. As a child growing up on Daufuskie, I had so much to be thankful for. We were always there for each other, no matter how tough times got. Momma and Pop used to tell us many stories about how hard things were for them when they were growing up, but how hard times never hurt them. Pop believed that a good, backbreaking day of work was good for you and made you stronger. A full belly, a good night's rest, and getting up with the chickens kept you going.

We never had as much as some but always had what was needed. Pop and Momma were known as two of a kind; they both worked hard and had big hearts, and they shared with everyone. When they started their life together, I was about four months old, as they united two already-made families, eight children (two boys and six girls), under one roof in a two-bedroom house. Two years later they added a set of twin girls of their own. Our sleeping space was tight. The boys slept on the couch or a pad on the floor, and we girls slept in a big bed pushed up against the wall.

Even though Pop and Momma had very little education, they knew what was important for our future: they taught us to do the right thing, and they encouraged us to get a good education. They made us study hard and do our homework before we did any yardwork or housework during the school term. Hard work, cleanliness, and manners will take you where money won't, they drilled into us and reminded us constantly.

Pop and Momma were always busy doing something. They didn't often stop to give us hugs or kisses or to say out loud they loved us. Their love was silent; it was tough love that taught us to survive. But everything they strived for and everything they encouraged us to do to better ourselves told us how much they truly loved us.

Their rules and discipline never changed for us, whether we lived at home or were grown and gone away. Give or take, right or wrong, they were the parents and we were the kids. Being grown meant being on your own; but, even so, if you were in their house, you respected and obeyed their rules. Pop never let us forget that although he wasn't book smart, he could rely on his mother wit, which made him smarter than we would ever be. He believed if it wasn't broke, you don't fix it: finding fault meant looking for trouble; fixing trouble took time; and time lost was time you could never get back. As kids growing up, our biggest challenge was to have patience and take one day at a time, realizing how important time was.

Pop and Momma only wanted the very best for all of us, and they worked hard to make it possible. We never knew how hard it was for them sometimes, day to day. There were times when we didn't understand why they worked so hard and pushed us so hard, but we didn't complain. They taught us good values, to be independent, to be leaders, and to do our best in all that we did. And they taught us to have faith and give thanks to our Heavenly Father. These lessons and others I can say we learned well. For teaching us these things, and more, they are my heroes.

So this book is in memory of a great Pop, Thomas Stafford Sr., who died August 3, 1988, a day before my birthday. I love you and thank you for all that you have taught me in your special way. You always made sure we paid attention so that things were done right, and your being there for us will never be forgotten.

And this book is for Mom, Albertha R. Stafford, a lady who has jumped through many hoops in her life. She still hangs in strong, even after suffering a stroke in 1997, a month after the death of her father, for whom she had cared for many years (after caring for her husband before that). She gives true meaning to the hymn, "May the Work I've Done Speak for Me." Even though her body has slowed down, her mental state is sharp, and she still lets us know that she is the cob and we are the corn. When we get together, we sometimes share memories of—and can't help laughing about—many of the moments we had with Pop and with other family and friends on Daufuskie. I am very proud be a "beenyah" (Daufuskie native) and to have lived on the island during the changes it has seen. I will always treasure every moment and everything we have shared and given to each other. Momma, I will love you always.

Momma and Pop were the inspiration, but this book would not have been possible without the support of other special folks as well.

Thanks to my loving kids—my first-born, Charles Edward Simmons IV, who died at the age of six in 1981, Jermaine Adonuise Robinson, Kecia Polite Robinson, Rakenya Niccole Robinson, Isiah Lamar Coleman, and Thomas Morris Bush—who have taught me about patience and unconditional love.

Thanks also to my precious grandkids, who call me Nana: Jaquasha Anreona Bush, Jermaine Adonuise Robinson Jr., Charmaine Jamira Robinson, Tanasha Aārielle Robinson, and Janaesha Kiona Robinson.

Very special thanks to Greg and Janet Smith and their kids and to Greg's mother. Thanks also to Bill Ferguson, who introduced me to the Smith family. Greg took the time to help me put this book together, sharing the work of writing and taking all of the photos that appear here. You made me a part of your family, and we learned from each other as we worked together. I enjoyed every moment and appreciate what each of you has given me. You are special people.

I can't say thank you enough to Captain Edward T. Harris, a great friend, for being there at a rough time and assuring me through all the changes in my life that I could do anything as long as I believed in myself. He encouraged me to share some of the secrets of my cooking with folks who wanted to know how it was done.

Many thanks to all my siblings—Thomas Stafford Jr., Lillian Mitchell, Sylvia Williams, Otis Stafford, Lascenay Young, Jeanetta L. Robinson, Catherine Gueye, Linda Marie Stafford, Lois Faye Stafford, Altrovies Latrell Ward, and Alton Ward Jr.—and my wonderful nieces and nephews.

For his wonderful love that gets me through the day, I thank Jeffrey W. Bacon Jr. I appreciate your spirit, motivation, and emotional support; you mean so much to me.

And for all my aunts, my cousins far and near, and friends old and new, thank you and may God bless you always.

Gullah Home Cooking *the* Daufuskie Way

INTRODUCTION

When midwife Sarah Grant rushed over the plank across the swamp near Grandmomma's some 40 years ago, she was about to bring me into a world very different from anything that exists today.

Married to Daufuskie's undertaker (the Grants got us coming and going, folks used to say) Miz Sarah was the last of our small island's midwives. Her world, the one she introduced me to, was set for some big changes—but not before I learned its ways.

Folks on our island had little money, but we had a thriving economy and a rich life. Unlike children today, my sisters and I didn't have a long list of things we wanted from somewhere and someone else. We didn't know about them. But what we did know—the yard, the garden, the woods, the river, and our community of neighbors—gave us all we needed, and, it seemed, all we could want. By the time I was grown, much of that, including most of our neighbors, would be gone.

ISLAND LIFE

The Sea Islands along the South Carolina and Georgia coasts—with their unique landscape, climate, culture, and history—have, time and again, caught and lost the attention of the world. Daufuskie is one of those small islands. From Bloody Point beach on its south end, you can see Tybee Island, Georgia; Hilton Head Island, South Carolina; and between them, the Atlantic Ocean. Without a bridge to either of those resort islands or the nearby mainland, Daufuskie is remote, yet it has always been within reach, just a short boat ride away.

Saltwater marshes wrap around the west and south sides of the island. Fish, crabs, shrimp, oysters, and just about every other sea life you can

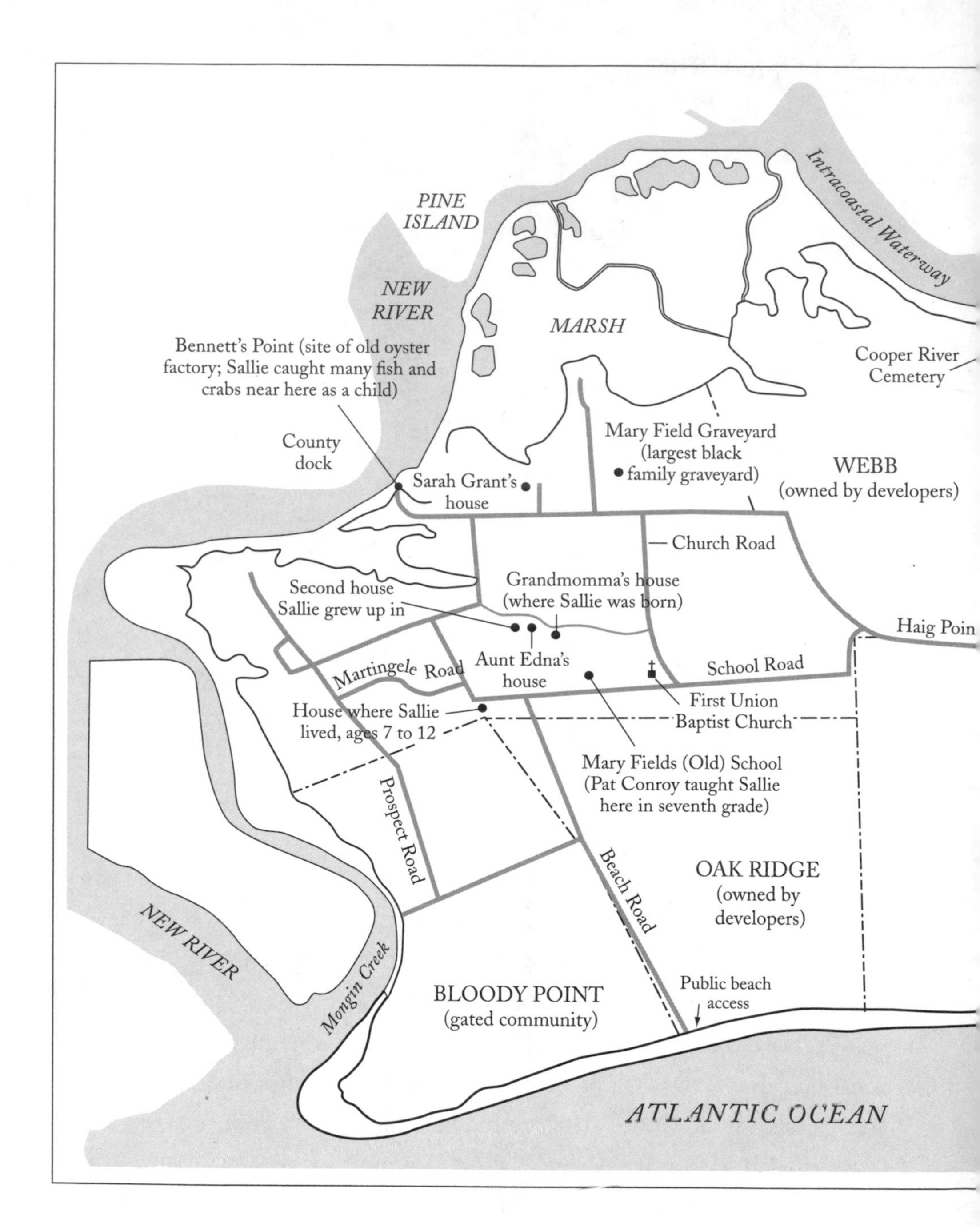

Daufuskie Island

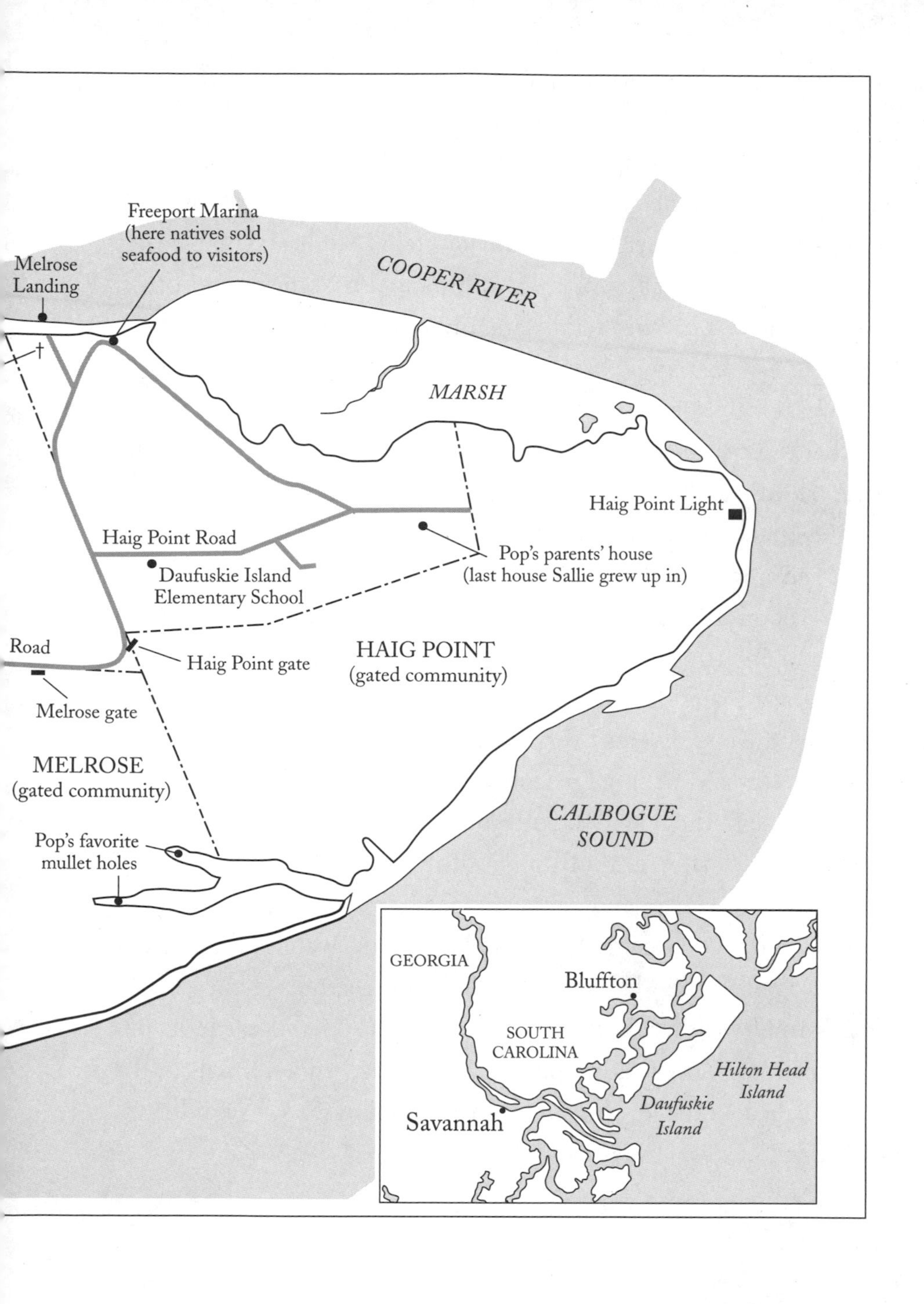

Freeport Marina
(here natives sold
seafood to visitors)
Melrose
Landing
COOPER RIVER
MARSH
Haig Point Light
Haig Point Road
Pop's parents' house
(last house Sallie grew up in)
Daufuskie Island
Elementary School
Road
Haig Point gate
HAIG POINT
(gated community)
Melrose gate
MELROSE
(gated community)
CALIBOGUE
SOUND
Pop's favorite
mullet holes
GEORGIA
Bluffton
SOUTH
CAROLINA
Hilton Head
Island
Daufuskie
Island
Savannah

imagine breed, grow, and live in the tidal creeks and rivers that snake through the marshes. Palmetto trees rattle in the breeze and stand against all but the meanest hurricane winds. Tall pines and ancient live oaks hold the mystery of generations gone in their beards of Spanish moss and frocks of resurrection ferns. Snakes, rabbits, coons, small island deer, foxes, and probably a few bobcats still wander the thick underbrush of sparkleberries, wax myrtle, and briars. Shopping trips—for all but the barest necessities—call for a boat.

Life moves a little slower.

And when I was coming up on 'Fuskie (as we call our home), life moved a *lot* slower. Running water, when I was a child, came from a hand pump in the kitchen or yard. Half the bathroom was out back: the other half was a galvanized washtub in the kitchen—or in the yard on a hot summer afternoon. If you didn't own a boat—and we didn't—you had to plan your shopping trips for when you could catch a ride. For a few years, there was a government-funded public ferry service aboard surplus military boats, but the boats weren't very reliable. Some of our neighbors had old, wooden bateaus with small motors that would putt along the creeks that wound through the marshes. And sometimes we could ride along or send a list to Messex store in Bluffton, South Carolina, where we kept an open account, or to Hester and Zipperer feed and seed in Savannah.

But most of our food came from the land—and water—around our tin-roofed home. We tended a big garden, four seasons of the year in Daufuskie's mild weather. We raised chickens, hogs, and cattle in our yard. We gathered berries and trapped or sometimes shot animals in the woods. We fished, crabbed, shrimped, and picked oysters. We didn't always have a lot, but we always had enough.

Daufuskie's ocean beach, looking south toward Bloody Point.

YONDAH TIMES

I remember so well my childhood days on Daufuskie in the 1960s and 1970s. While the rest of the country was fighting over civil rights and the war in Vietnam, we were living much the way our great-grandparents had at the turn of the century. While kids elsewhere watched TV or went to the movies, we listened to the Supremes and the Temptations on battery-powered radios under the glow of oil lamps.

It's not as if the world never knew Daufuskie. Off and on, the island has played important economic, even historic, roles. But when I was coming up, the world was dancing, for the most part, without us.

Records of life on Daufuskie date back to the late 1600s, when European explorers began building settlements in the rich woods of the South Carolina Lowcountry. On Daufuskie and other islands, they found shell rings and mounds left by forgotten Native Americans. Bloody Point, the island's southeast corner, earned its name in a pair of battles during the Yemassee War in the early 1700s. After the defeated Yemassee Indians left the area for Florida, colonial planters shipped timber, indigo, and cotton back to England to fuel the Industrial Revolution. During the American Revolution, Daufuskie's Tory planters, loyal to the British king, raided the plantations of patriots on nearby Hilton Head, and were, in turn, attacked by the patriots.

Daufuskie grew quickly as part of the young United States. Plantations, built by slaves and cut off by water from the rest of the world, grew timber, cotton, and the unique Gullah culture. The Civil War ended the plantation economy, but the Gullah people stayed, farming the subdivided lands of former plantations and fishing the creeks around the island.

During the last years of the nineteenth century and the early part of the twentieth century, Daufuskie was an important stop for ferries that cruised the inland waters around the Sea Islands of South Carolina. An oyster canning factory at Bennett's Point made the island somewhat fa-

Sallie checks her watch as she walks down still-unpaved School Road, following the same route she did after school during much of her childhood. (The ruins of the house where she lived from ages 7 to 12 are just ahead and to her left, back in what is now thick woods.)

Pop's house on Haig Point Road, where Sallie spent the last of her teenage years. The rusting wagon skeleton is from the same wagon that Bobby the cow used to pull.

mous. (You can still buy "Daufuski" brand oysters in red cans that are now packed in Korea.) Folks, mostly the descendants of slaves, had jobs at that factory, timbering, or on the boats that hauled oysters, fish, produce, and people. Others farmed their land, trading vegetables, eggs, and meat for goods at several island stores. The stores would sell the produce to other islanders—as well as to folks on the mainland. My grandfather worked for years, at a dollar a day, on a dredge that kept the inland creeks open. At one point, more than 1,000 people lived on Daufuskie. Few folks got much ahead, but most got by.

In the 1950s, growing industry along the nearby Savannah River polluted many of the marshes and creeks around Daufuskie. Health officials closed most of the valuable oyster beds. There was little work and almost no money, so most folks left the island. One by one, the stores closed.

Islanders who stayed, like my parents and grandparents, loved Daufuskie and its laid-back living. Some folks knew well that corn was good for making more than meal and grapes for making more than jelly. The easy island lifestyle slowed even more. When I was a child, no more than 200 people remained on the island. Two thriving churches dwindled to one struggling parish. The two-room Mary Field School struggled to educate several dozen children, including me, through the eighth grade. White folks, other than rich men who came to hunt and fish in the winter, were few.

TIMES COME A CHANGIN'

When I was in the seventh grade, Pat Conroy, then a young, idealistic teacher, came down from Beaufort (the seat of Beaufort County, South Carolina, which includes Daufuskie) to help Miz Johnson, our local teacher. He taught us things in ways we could never have imagined—and I will never forget. We learned about outer space through a telescope. Instead of having us sit in the classroom all day, he would quiz

Grandmomma's house on Bryan Road, where Sallie was born and spent many youthful afternoons.

us as we ran down the beach. He took us on field trips to Washington, to see the Harlem Globetrotters in Savannah, and to go trick or treating in Beaufort. We acted out *A Christmas Carol*, instead of just reading it. The words in our books described a wide world we couldn't see from Daufuskie. Pat showed it to us.

All this didn't sit well with Miz Johnson or the Beaufort County School District. But it did change our lives, and for Conroy the experience resulted in the novel *The Water Is Wide*, which was made into the movie "Conrack."

But with or without Pat Conroy, life on Daufuskie was about to change again. Although my family and many others like us owned property on the island, several large plantation properties remained mostly intact. The owners, who lived hundreds or thousands of miles away, grew timber and leased the properties for hunting. But as my sisters and I were growing up, so was nearby Hilton Head. Real estate developers looked across the water at Daufuskie and saw an island that seemed perfect for exclusive resorts, spas, golf courses, riding stables, and big profits. By the mid-1980s, two large properties—Melrose and Haig Point plantations—were under development.

I remember my mother fussing at big trucks as they rumbled by the house, spraying dust on her freshly hung laundry. Big houses sprang up on small lots, laid out along freshly turned sand that would soon be golf courses. Horses came back to the island, but the new animals lived in fancy stables, ate fancy feed, and had fancy saddles. Ferry service returned, but unless you were a property owner or a club member or employee, you usually weren't welcome aboard. Tour boats came, telling their passengers tall tales of island life.

Although a few of us worked for our new neighbors, more islanders, especially the young, left to find jobs and schools across the water. I left (although I plan to move back), as did most of our neighbors and all but a few of our relatives. Only a couple dozen native islanders remain. Some of these folks still sell their famous deviled crabs, as we did when I was a child, to tourists as they come ashore on the Bennett's Point or Cooper River docks.

If you have patience and a sharp eye, you can still find prehistoric sharks' teeth and arrowheads along the eroding shores of Daufuskie. And along the back roads of the island, you can still hear a few folks talking in the rhythms of Gullah. But even as that blend of African and English is washing away like the shore, you can still have a taste of 'Fuskie in a forkful of Pop's smuttered mullet or Sea Island okra gumbo.

Food is life. And the way we lived, life was gathering, growing, and preparing food. For some readers, the tales and recipes in this book will seem like memories. For others, they'll be discoveries. But whether you grew up in a high-rise or a tin-roofed shack, the meals described here will sho'nuff stick to your ribs.

If there's one thing we learned coming up on Daufuskie, it's the importance of good, home-cooked food. Ingredients were plentiful on our island, but (except for the very old, the very young, the sick, and the shut-in) we had to earn our meals. Without our hard work—growing, gathering, and catching—we had nothing much for our table.

That doesn't mean anyone went hungry. If you were walking down a road or path and smelled the 'roma of fresh cornbread, lima beans, and fried chicken, you could follow your nose to a good meal. And you were always welcome. Sharing from one hand to another made good meals available to all.

'Fuskie folks have known their way 'round the stove for generations. But while most all of us in my family were cooks from the time we could see over the edge of the stove, Momma ran the kitchen. She would fix up a big breakfast and usually cooked our afternoon dinner, which we would eat between 3:00 and 5:00, depending on the day's work. Most times, we didn't have any lunch, or if we did, it was just a snack. If Momma wasn't home, was tired of cooking, or didn't want to cook what we wanted to eat, Pop, my sisters, or I might cook dinner. Pop especially liked to cook shrimp and fish still jumping from his "mullet hole" in the creek.

Even though he cooked himself, Pop always reminded us cooking was woman's work. "If ya wanna keep ya a good man," he used to tell my sisters and me, "ya gotta know how to cook a good meal."

We planned most meals a day or more ahead because we had to gather and prepare the ingredients before we could fix the meal. We also had to cut and haul wood for the stove and pump water, carrying full buckets inside. We kept a stack of firewood drying behind the stove, and five-gallon buckets of water, covered with lids, sat on the corner table near the stove. After dinner, we refilled the buckets and brought in more wood so Momma would have supplies handy for breakfast.

There was a season for almost everything: a time to catch different seafood, a time to butcher the hog or cow, a time to plant and harvest each crop, a time for hunting each animal. Each nut, fruit, and berry ripened in its own time.

And it was always firewood season. Keeping our stove hot was no small chore. Every two weeks or so, we hitched Bobby the cow to the wagon and headed, as a family, into the woods. Pop swung his ax to chop deep into the trees on the side where he wanted them to fall. My sisters and I took turns at either end of our big, crosscut saw. We cut the trees down, then into sections that fit our wagon. If Momma didn't have to tend a meal cooking at home, she helped, too, picking up pine branches and cones for kindling, and loading the firewood. There was still more work when we got the wood home. We had to cut it into usable logs, stack them, and carry in wood for the evening meal. These chores would last nearly all day, summer and winter. Of course, we needed more wood for heat in the winter, but the cookstove had to be fired up year-round.

Getting food from the store—such as the big sacks of flour, grits, and rice that were our staples—meant hitching Bobby to the wagon, riding down to the landing, tying Bobby to a tree near some good grass, and boarding the ferry or a neighbor's boat. On the other side—Savannah, Hilton Head Island, or the small town of Bluffton—we had to find a ride to the store and one back to the landing. Then, after a long boat ride, at the end of a long day, we had to hitch up Bobby, load the wagon, and head home along dirt roads.

We weren't wealthy, but we were well fed and we were certainly clean. We washed ourselves, with Momma making sure we scrubbed every nook and cranny. We washed our pots, dishes, forks, and spoons with

An old woodstove sits ready with wood and wash pans nearby in a Daufuskie home. Sallie's grandmother, as well as many friends and relatives, had similar stoves, although her family's was bigger.

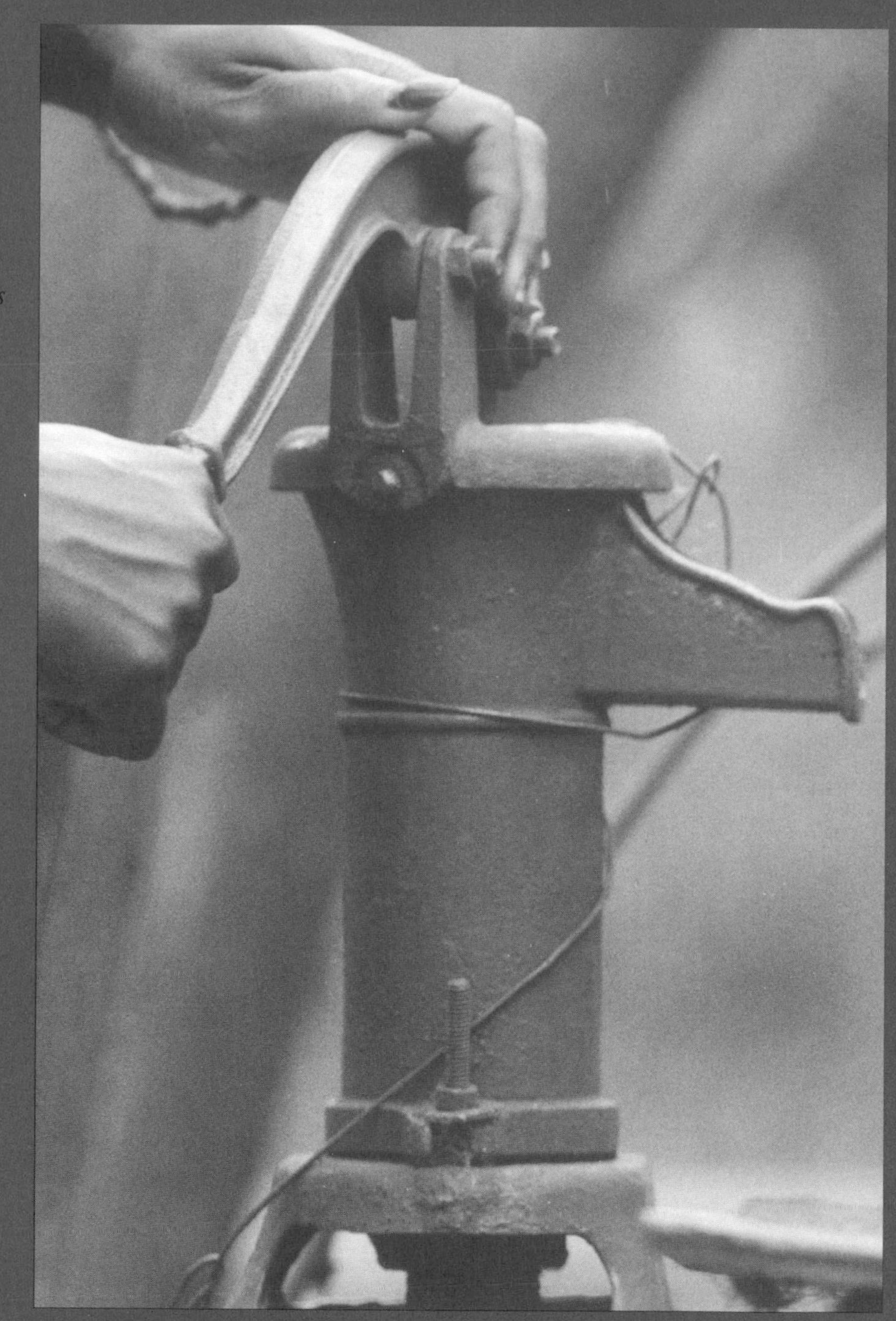

A hand pump on Daufuskie, similar to the pumps that were near Sallie's childhood homes and in several kitchens.

water heated on the stove. And when black soot from our woodstove built up on our pots, Momma would send us out back to shine them with sand and crumbled bricks. We washed all our food completely before cooking. And we cooked everything thoroughly. Our meat wasn't pink, and our vegetables weren't crunchy.

We worked hard and we got dirty. But when we got up each morning, we put on clean clothes. "Ya nevah know who gonna drop by," Momma would say, as we gathered the dirty clothes and she boiled up water in a big, black pot out back. Twice a week, Momma made us take turns scrubbing clothes on the washboard and hanging them on her half dozen clotheslines strung across the side yard. Then we had to heat the heavy iron on the stove and press our frocks on her homemade ironing board, propped between a chair and a table, in the kitchen. Flour and water boiled on the stove on laundry days, and we stirred it constantly, so our "starch" didn't lump up.

Although Pop would cook his fish whenever he wanted it, Momma usually started dinner right after breakfast. We called such meals "long pots." Many of the recipes in this book can be cooked that way, for several hours over low to medium heat, which was just about the only kind our woodstove gave us. Momma would join the rest of us when we worked near the house. But if the day's work wasn't in the yard, the nearby fields, or the woods, we were on our own, because she couldn't leave the stove untended. When all our chores were done for the day, we didn't have to wait for our dinner.

As my parents used to say, hard work and a little sweat never hurt anyone. And they didn't hurt me—much. I remember the play that mixed with our chores, the good ol' 'romas from the kitchen, and how a good, hardy meal filled my empty belly.

SPOKEN LANGUAGE ON DAUFUSKIE

In the past 20 years, Gullah-'Geechee culture and language have drawn lots of attention. Professors have researched how English and African phrases mixed on the Sea Islands along the Georgia and South Carolina coasts. African leaders have visited St. Helena Island (a dozen miles, by water, north of Daufuskie), highlighting the connections between continents and peoples. Annual gatherings in Beaufort, on Hilton Head Island, and on Georgia's Sapelo Island celebrate a fading language and way of life.

But my sisters and I never knew we were Gullah. I remember the first time some tourists asked me if I could speak Gullah. I asked back, "What be dat?"

For most of my life, I've tried to adjust the way I speak to the folks I'm speaking to. Day to day, I measure every phrase before I say it, and some things just don't come out right. But when I get back with 'Fuskie folks, my words come easily.

My grandfather, Josephus Robinson, was a small, quiet man. But he did tell us stories. He spoke in quick, short phrases, often mumbled through a chaw of tobacco. Folks born on the island were "beenyahs." Folks from across the water were "comeyahs." The word "that" was "dat." "Them" was "dem." He didn't "remember"; he would "famemba." A burlap bag—which we would use for all sorts of things—was a "croaker sack." And although our Gullah was thinned out by what we heard on the radio and learned in school, we understood every word.

"'Til ya been ova deh," he would explain, "ya jus' don' know." And he was always right—wherever "ova deh" was. It could be across the water, across the path, or across the room. And when someone asked directions, the answer was always "down yondah" with a finger pointed toward wherever "yondah" was.

Tales of many years past started with "back in dem days," while "da

Sallie walks down a dock ramp (carrying an antique iron that she used as a child) toward a workers' ferry at Freeport Marina on Daufuskie.

other day" could be two days or two years gone by. Sometimes young people were "chillen." Other times, we were "churn." Pop would "trow" his net, not "throw" it. And we understood.

But folks from "ova deh" couldn't understand us. We learned early to be careful with our words. In school, Miz Johnson, who was from somewhere to the north, made an example of me. I was a tomboy, I slouched in my chair, I didn't cross my legs like a lady, and I didn't talk right. She would grab me by the ear and drag me to the front of the room. I would have to rephrase whatever I had just said incorrectly, as backs straightened against every chair in the room.

But Miz Johnson, who was a big woman and fairly scary to us, also let me know she was hard on me for a reason. "Sallie Ann," she would say, "you're a smart girl, and I see so much in you. You can do better. Now pay attention."

And sometimes she used me as a good example for older kids, telling them that if I could do the math problem or spell the word, so could they. There was a world beyond Daufuskie, she explained to tired (and sore!) ears. And we needed to be ready for it.

For good or ill, she was right.

RECIPES AND MEASUREMENTS

I keep a clean kitchen, but I have to admit there's dust on the measuring spoons hanging beside my stove. We never had a measuring cup or kitchen scale, and I don't use either when I cook. We did have pork-and-beans cans for scooping flour, rice, and grits from the big covered galvanized tins under the kitchen table. But a can full wasn't a measurement. A "scoop" was. It was less than a full can, dependent on the cook's eye and hand. And that has made writing down our family recipes quite a challenge.

I learned most of the recipes in this book at Momma's and Pop's sides

Grandmomma's kitchen, much as Sallie's mother left it, when she moved from the house in 1996.

as they added a "pour" or a "pench" or a "dash" of this or that to a pot or bowl. Few meals mixed up the same way twice. Momma might try adding some thyme or garlic powder to a long pot that had been seasoned before with just salt and pepper.

But over the years, both she and I have fallen into patterns of cooking. We have versions of recipes we like better than others. A key challenge in writing this book has been translating those measured handfuls into cups and dashes into tablespoons. But hear me: for us, these crude measures were consistent. Momma could measure out ten handfuls of hamburger, and I'll bet you there wouldn't be an ounce of difference between them.

I don't cook all these recipes regularly. Possum is not a staple in my house. I wouldn't cook it in my pot. And then there's okra. The other day, I was shopping for frozen butter beans, and I picked up a package of cut okra by mistake. When I read the label, I dropped the bag on the floor. I don't like okra. I just can't tolerate the smell—let alone the slime. But my writing partner, Greg (whose mother makes a mean batch of gumbo), loves it, and it is a standard ingredient in Southern cooking.

Most recipes in this book (with the exception of many of those for breads and desserts, since most such recipes are based on pan sizes rather than servings) should feed four to six people, which was about the number of folks we usually had at our table. In many cases, you can adjust the quantities of ingredients proportionally for more or fewer servings. But please treat such adjustments as experiments, since smaller or larger batches may require fiddling with proportions.

In short, these are recipes, not rules. We cook creatively. And I hope you will, too. Stir, taste, add a dash, stir, and taste some more. I'm sure you can enjoy these recipes just as they're written. But the real joy comes from fixin' and mixin' on your own.

Here are my family's recipes. Please make them yours.

HEALTHIER FIXIN' & MIXIN'

Southern cooking has earned a bad reputation among many health advocates. And there is some reason for concern. High blood pressure, diabetes, heart disease, and strokes are more common in the South, particularly among African Americans, than elsewhere in the United States.

One reason may be that our cooking traditions come from a time when folks worked hard all day under a hot, Southern sun. These days, most of us just don't burn off fat and calories the way many Southerners used to.

Still, we like our fatback, fried chicken, and peach cobbler. All of us just can't all eat these things. What's a Southern cook to do?

First, you can ease up on some ingredients. Cooking with a third less sugar and fat won't do too much damage to most of the recipes in this book. Similarly, you can cut some or all of the added salt from most of these dishes. And either salt or sugar substitutes can make up for some of the flavor lost.

But the single biggest step you can take to make recipes healthier is to manage—not necessarily eliminate—the fats you use for cooking. Bacon grease can be replaced with a healthy vegetable oil and, if you like, soy bean–based "bacon bits" or artificial bacon flavoring. Where we used lard (cooked-down pork fat) or tallow (beef fat) for cooking, you can use peanut, canola, sunflower, or olive oil, as I usually do these days. Each of these vegetable oils has its own flavor and response to heat, but all are low in bad cholesterol.

Where the recipes list butter as an ingredient, you can use a "light" margarine. A light coating of Pam, or a similar cooking spray, can replace several tablespoons of oil in a pan. And if you cook with nonstick pans, you can nearly eliminate fat and oil from stir-frying and sautéing.

Salted meats can be replaced with smoked turkey products or even bacon bits in some recipes. Removing the skin from poultry gets rid of much of the fat. Cornstarch will thicken gravy, even if you've skimmed off all the fat, nearly as well as flour and oil. Instead of cooking with fatty meats, choose leaner cuts and marinate them for tenderness and flavor.

Bake, steam, or poach instead of frying to cut calories and fat. Steam your vegetables just past crunchy to preserve vitamins. You can also replace white flour and white rice with whole-wheat flour and brown rice in many of these recipes to get more fiber and vitamins and to avoid chemicals used in bleaching processes.

And if you want to avoid processed sugar, you have many choices. Honey and other raw sugars are better for some folks. You can sweeten many cakes, pies, and puddings with natural sugars, using apple juice, pear juice, or crushed pineapple. You can also use chemical sugar substitutes, but read the labels, since some can change when cooked.

Oil and vinegar, perhaps with a dash of sweetener, can replace mayonnaise in salads. Low-cholesterol egg substitutes work fine in many recipes, and cutting the yolk from boiled eggs still lets you add hard-boiled egg whites to a low-cholesterol potato salad.

Remember, this book is about fixin' and mixin'. Every generation has added something to these recipes. And some cooks have removed things. Don't hesitate to mix up versions that suit your own tastes and needs.

I

salads

We didn't grow lettuce. But we had salads.

To us, a chilled mixture of ingredients, usually including some mayonnaise, was a salad. We used fresh fruits and vegetables, well-cooked meats and fish, and even some ingredients from cans and boxes.

Most salads were extras for a Sunday meal that already included meat, cooked vegetables, and rice. They were usually light summer dishes that didn't require the woodstove—although some of the ingredients might have been cooked. Leftovers often found their way into salads. If there was a community gathering, you can bet many of the covered dishes held salads inside.

Although the following recipes are fairly precise, we weren't strict about what we made salads with or how we made them. Every salad was a creative project. Momma would add a little of this, taste, then add some of that.

I like egg and pickles in my salads, and you'll find plenty of hard-boiled eggs and sweet pickle relish in the following pages. Other folks like more mustard or mayonnaise than I do. Many of these recipes include onions, but I often leave them out, because the salad keeps better without them.

In short, good salad makers aren't afraid to experiment a little. Please take these recipes as inspiration, then fix and mix to your heart's content.

NUT AND APPLE SALAD

6–8 apples
½ cup raisins
½ cup chopped nuts (walnuts or pecans)
½ cup celery, chopped
mayonnaise (desired amount)

Wash the apples, cut in half, core, and dice. Combine all the ingredients in a bowl. Chill or eat right away. But be sure to keep the salad cool, because the apples will get soft at room temperature.

TOSSED COLESLAW

1 small head cabbage
1–2 medium carrots
½ cup vinegar
½ cup vegetable oil
salt and black pepper to taste

Peel the outer layer of cabbage and discard; wash and drain the remaining head and cut it into quarters. Shred the cabbage and carrots into a medium bowl. Add the vinegar, oil, salt, and pepper. Toss together well. Chill at least 45 minutes to let the flavor come through.

HAND-PICKED CUCUMBER AND TOMATO SALAD

This is a quick and easy summer salad, without lettuce or other cool-weather crops. The seasoning is simple, so it highlights the flavors of fresh produce.

2–4 cucumbers, sliced
3 tomatoes, cut into wedges
1 small onion, cut into rings
½ cup vinegar
¼ cup vegetable oil
salt and black pepper to taste

Wash the vegetables thoroughly. Cut the cucumber, tomatoes, and onion as indicated, and place in a bowl. Add the vinegar, oil, salt, and pepper. Combine, then chill or serve immediately.

MIXED FRUIT AND NUT SALAD

When we were coming up, we had pear, apple, peach, persimmon, mulberry, walnut, and pecan trees growing in either our yard or our neighbors'. We also grew scuppernong grapes and all kinds of melons, and we gathered wild blackberries, blueberries, fox grapes, and nuts from the fields and woods. Sometimes Momma, on her trips to a mainland grocery store, would pick up bananas, green grapes, oranges, grapefruit, or apples. This was especially true around Christmas, since fruit was a traditional gift for children.

During the spring and summer months, fruits were plentiful, and each had its season. First came the blackberries and blueberries in early June, then the peaches, plums, and grapes. Persimmons, pears, and apples ripened in late summer, followed by the walnuts and pecans in the late fall. Like any children, we were impatient. We watched eagerly as buds blossomed and grew into sweet treats. In turn, Momma and Pop watched us closely to keep us from stealing the fruit early before it ripened on the trees and vines. But when they were away, we would sneak green pears and apples or even pecans that weren't quite ripe. And, sure enough, we would eat too much and get sick. And we would get caught. And we would have to swallow doses of castor oil, which Pop called the "flushin' medicine."

Still, once the fruit was ripe, Momma was happy to give it to us as a snack, saying, "Disyah will tie y'all ovah 'til dinnah." And when it was ripe, she and Pop counted on us for labor. The hogs, cattle, birds, and squirrels all loved the fruit, too. And most of the fruit ripened just about the time Pop plowed the summer garden under and let the animals loose to root through the turned soil for missed potatoes, garden scraps, and grubs. It was our job to pick the ripened fruit off the ground before the animals could get it or it rotted.

Momma loved to make both pear and watermelon rind preserves to get us through the winter, as well as fruit breads, cobblers, and pies that we ate in season. But when fruits were plentiful in mid- to late summer, she would often mix up a bowl of fruit salad. What a cool treat it was on a hot summer day, and Momma was pleased because it was all natural and good for us.

4–6 cups total of at least 2 or 3 kinds of fresh fruit
½ cup chopped pecans and/or walnuts

Combine equal amounts of the fruit—any type of sweet fruit is great, so Momma used whatever we had, such as peaches, pears, blueberries, blackberries, apples, grapes, watermelon, cantaloupe, and mulberries—with the nuts. Chill and serve.

TADA SALAD

6–8 white potatoes (more or less, depending on size)
4–5 eggs
1 stalk celery, diced
½ medium green bell pepper, diced
½ medium red bell pepper, diced
½ medium onion, chopped (optional)
½ teaspoon paprika
⅓ cup sweet pickle cubes
1 teaspoon prepared yellow mustard
1 tablespoon hot sauce (optional)
⅓ cup mayonnaise (more or less to taste)
salt and black pepper to taste

Peel the potatoes or leave the skins on, depending on your preference. Wash them and dice into ¾-inch cubes. Place the potatoes and eggs in a medium pot, half filled with salted water. Boil gently 10 to 20 minutes, until the potatoes are cooked firm, not mushy. Remove the potatoes, place in a bowl, and allow to cool, leaving the eggs to boil a few

Chopping vegetables in Sallie's kitchen.

minutes longer. Drain the eggs and chill in cold water. Peel the eggs and dice. When the potatoes are cool, add the celery, green pepper, red pepper, onion, and paprika. Gently combine. Add the eggs, sweet pickle, mustard, hot sauce, and mayonnaise. Combine well. Add salt and pepper to taste.

MOMMA'S SHRIMP AND TADA SALAD

This is a recipe that feeds my beenyah soul. It's simple, but when you work from raw ingredients, as we did, it's a project. We had to catch the shrimp, then head, peel (shell), and devein them. Potatoes had to be planted, tended, dug, washed, peeled, cut, and boiled. And all the other ingredients had to be bought, grown, or collected. The sea and the garden, as well as all we did to harvest from both, come together in what remains one of my favorite dishes.

I remember shrimp and tada salad filling my favorite bowl on Momma's Sunday dinner table. And my kids still beg me to fix it for them. Trouble is, I have to beg them to peel the shrimp. I still can't bring myself to buy precooked, frozen shrimp, but this recipe will work with them, too.

2 cups medium shrimp, peeled and deveined
5–6 medium potatoes, peeled and diced
5–6 eggs
½ medium green bell pepper
½ medium red bell pepper
1 stalk celery
1–2 teaspoons prepared yellow mustard
1–2 teaspoons garlic powder

1 teaspoon thyme (ground or leaves)
½ cup sweet pickle relish
sprinkle paprika
hot sauce (optional—if you like it hot!)
⅓–½ cup mayonnaise (more or less to taste)

Add the shrimp to boiling, salted water and cook 2 to 3 minutes (cook too long and they'll get chewy, then mushy). Boil the diced potatoes separately or in the shrimp water 10 to 15 minutes, until tender but still firm. Boil the eggs until hard (10 to 15 minutes). Allow all to cool while you dice the peppers and celery. Dice the eggs and combine all of the ingredients, adding the mayonnaise last, so you can control the texture of the salad. Chill and serve over a bed of lettuce or other fresh greens.

BLOSSOM'S CHICKEN SALAD

Grandmomma, whom everybody but us called "Blossom," used to say a chicken was good for more than just frying, baking, or smothering in a sauce.

"Hona chil', I kin tell ya, 'cause I fo' know," she'd say. "Ah been cookin' all mah days, an' Ah know dem chickens in dat yard." And sho'nuff, she had a particular pullet in mind when she set out to make chicken salad. She would walk into the coop, toss some cracked corn at her feet, and watch the chickens rush in around her. She would spot her bird, usually a young, plump one, grab it by the base of its wings, lift it up, and get a good hold on its legs. This would swing the chicken upside down and limit its flapping. Then she would shake it, so it dropped its wings to show just how plump it was and so she could guess its weight. If Grandmomma didn't like what she saw, or what she felt with her practiced hands, she would toss the bird aside and choose another.

And, of course, she always chose well. She invested time, energy, and plenty of cracked corn in raising her birds, and she had a plan for each one, from laying box to frying pan.

Chicken salad was a side dish or a heavy snack for us. But it makes a great meal, as well.

1 chicken (about 1½ pounds)
1 stalk celery, diced
1 small onion, finely diced
½ medium green bell pepper, diced
½ cup sweet pickle relish
½ teaspoon garlic powder
½ teaspoon paprika
½ teaspoon ground thyme (optional)
3–4 hard-boiled eggs, chopped
1 tablespoon prepared yellow mustard
⅓–½ cup mayonnaise (more or less to taste)

Take a whole chicken, cut it into parts, season it (if you like), put it in a pan, and bake in a preheated oven at 350° for 30 to 40 minutes, until thoroughly cooked. Let the chicken cool, then debone it and chop into ¾-inch cubes. Add the celery, onion, bell pepper, sweet relish, garlic powder, paprika, thyme, and eggs. Toss together, then stir in the mustard and mayonnaise. Chill in the refrigerator for at least 45 minutes so the flavors combine. Serve on a bed of lettuce, in a sandwich, or however you like.

TURKEY SALAD

2–3 cups chopped turkey (white and/or dark meat)
4–5 hard-boiled eggs, diced
⅓ cup sweet pickle cubes
1 stalk celery, diced
1 small green bell pepper, diced
1 small onion, diced
1 teaspoon black pepper
⅓–½ cup mayonnaise (more or less to taste)

Put the chopped turkey into a bowl. Add the eggs, sweet pickle, celery, bell pepper, onion, and black pepper. Stir in the mayonnaise, combine well, and go for it, chilled or not.

SALLIE'S SEAFOOD SALAD

As always, the right combination of ingredients makes a great dish.

1 pound medium shrimp
1 stalk celery, diced
½ small onion, diced
½ small green bell pepper, diced
1 teaspoon diced garlic
⅓ cup sweet pickle cubes
1 teaspoon prepared yellow mustard
½ teaspoon ground thyme
½ pound lump crabmeat

4 hard-boiled eggs, peeled and diced
½ cup mayonnaise (more or less to taste)
lettuce for bedding

In a pot half filled with salted water, boil the shrimp until pink, then 1 to 2 minutes longer. Drain the shrimp and allow to cool, then peel and devein. In a bowl, combine the celery, onion, bell pepper, garlic, sweet pickle, mustard, and thyme. Add the shrimp, crabmeat, and eggs. Combine gently, adding mayonnaise to reach the desired texture. Chill and serve on a bed of lettuce.

CAST NET SHRIMP SALAD

1½ pounds shrimp
¼ cup sweet pickle cubes
½ medium green bell pepper, diced
1 small onion, diced
½ stalk celery, diced
½ teaspoon ground thyme
4 hard-boiled eggs, peeled and diced
1 teaspoon prepared yellow mustard
⅓–½ cup mayonnaise (more or less to taste)
sprinkle of paprika
black pepper to taste
lettuce for bedding

In a pot half filled with salted water, boil the shrimp until pink, then 1 to 2 minutes longer. Drain the shrimp and allow to cool, then peel, devein, and place in a bowl. Add the sweet pickle, bell pepper, onion, celery, thyme, and eggs. Combine gently. Stir in the mustard, mayonnaise, paprika, and black pepper. Chill and serve on a bed of lettuce.

ISLANDER CRAB SALAD

Blue crabs have always been an important source of food and income for people along the southeastern coast. And folks on 'Fuskie are no exception. Crabmeat was a staple for our family, except in the coldest months, and it's still that way for many folks, rich and poor. Commercial crabbers work the waters around Daufuskie, and many families tend their own crab traps.

Like other islanders, we often kept a wire trap dangling from the public dock. Most nights during the warmer months, we would set it out. And most mornings, we'd find crabs—sometimes a dozen or more—inside it, ready for a boiling-hot bath in Pop's old washtub. Any family member headed to the dock carried fish or chicken scraps to bait the trap and a basket for collecting the crabs.

Nothing beats crabbing for entertaining the chillen. We used store-bought drop nets, when we had them. They sat flat on the river bottom, bait in the middle, and when we lifted the nets, they took on a bowl shape, trapping the crabs with the bait. We also crabbed with a chicken neck or fish head on a weighted cotton twine. Momma or Pop would gently slip a scoop net beneath the crabs we felt tugging on our lines.

Once we had caught a basket of crabs, we had to gather and stack firewood for Pop. He would rinse the crabs in fresh water, then start a fire under the big oak tree. When the fire was ready, he'd put an old washtub, a quarter full with salted water, on to boil. You cook crabs live, so we'd dump them into the boiling water and let them cook 10 minutes.

Picking the meat off the crabs was usually a family project. For most recipes, we'd mix the lump and claw meat, and that's true for islander crab salad.

2 cups crabmeat
½ medium onion, chopped
½ medium green bell pepper, chopped
3 hard-boiled eggs, peeled and diced
½ teaspoon ground thyme
½ teaspoon garlic powder
⅓ cup sweet pickle relish
black pepper to taste
⅓ cup mayonnaise (more or less to taste)
lettuce for bedding
celery tops for garnish (optional)
sprinkle paprika

Place the crabmeat in a bowl. Add the onion, bell pepper, eggs, thyme, garlic powder, sweet relish, black pepper, and mayonnaise. Combine thoroughly, but gently to avoid bruising the crab. Serve over lettuce with celery tops as a garnish and sprinkle with paprika. Be sure to refrigerate until eating time.

TUNA AND MACARONI SALAD

½ cup dry macaroni
2 6-ounce cans tuna
⅓ cup sweet pickle relish
½ medium green bell pepper, diced
½ medium onion, diced
½ stalk celery, diced
½ teaspoon ground thyme
½ teaspoon garlic powder
3–4 hard-boiled eggs, diced
¼–⅓ cup mayonnaise (more or less to taste)

Fill a medium pot halfway with salted water and bring to a rolling boil. Add the macaroni and cook until tender, not mushy. Drain, rinse in cool water, and set aside to cool. Open the tuna, drain off the oil or water, and combine with the cooled macaroni. Add the remaining ingredients. Stir to combine and chill until ready to eat. Serve alone or on a bed of lettuce.

2

The Garden

As little girls, we loved dirt. We loved the way it felt between our toes. We loved to sift sandy soil through our fingers. We loved to dig and build "sand houses" with dirt and lumber scraps. We loved to get dirty. And we loved to make mud pies—and even pretend to eat them, sometimes tasting with our tongues.

But dirt was much more than fun for us and a nuisance for Momma, who had to clean our clothes—and us. For generations, Daufuskie dirt fed our family. No, it wasn't on our menu, but the island's rich, sandy soil nourished a large share of what we ate—from the berry bushes in the woods, to the grass our animals ate, to the garden we tended most months of the year.

Around Christmas, Momma and Pop would pick up an Old Farmer's Almanac at Hester and Zipperer feed and seed in Savannah, then use it to help guide the planting of their crop. We usually put in our spring crop in early March, but if the groundhog had seen his shadow—that is, if we'd had a sunny February 2—we waited until the end of March.

As the late winter days grew longer, folks would start talking about the coming year's crops. The first step for Momma and Pop was to send us girls under the house to get the old tools. Our parents would burn or pound out rotted or broken handles on the hoes, rakes, and shovels, then drive in new handles we made together from small trees. Pop knew just the right trees to cut, just how much we should shave off with our old, two-handled plane, and just how long a green handle needed to dry before he pounded it into an old hoe.

A day or two before we plowed and planted, Pop would park himself on the corner of the porch with his flat file and a pile of garden tools. He'd lock his legs around a handle to hold it; then, in careful, angled strokes, Pop would sharpen every hoe so it cleanly sliced the roots off weeds with an "easy stroke."

We rotated our garden areas. And during the winter, we would tie the cows to stakes where we would plant most of our vegetables, then add chicken manure to their droppings. Every few years, we moved the hog pen, and we always grew good collards where the hogs had made their home. Some years, we broke new ground, clearing out small trees that had grown up. Pop would use a heavy "grub hoe" to cut and dig up the roots. We girls followed after him, pulling the roots from the dirt and piling them to burn.

We got dirty. But no dirtier than we would get the next few days, plowing and planting.

All our days started early, but I remember "gittin' up wi' da chickens" those first days of spring. We had to feed those chickens, slop the hogs, put the cows in the old field, pump water, and gather wood, yet still be in the garden as the morning dew burned off. Pop also insisted we get our work done before "dat sun git ova ya haid" and too hot. Dirt wasn't play for us on those days. It was work.

First, Pop would hitch Bobby the cow to our old, but freshly sharpened plow. He would let us take turns, so we learned how to hold the plow handles, along with the reins that guided the cow. We pulled them left or right to keep Bobby on a straight path, "unfolding" the dirt in even rows. Next we hoed those rows into hills that lined up across the garden. Momma and Pop would hoe out holes every foot or so. We followed behind, placing two or three seeds in each hole. Folks on Daufuskie believed that seeds planted by children and pregnant women would grow better.

The chores didn't end with planting. As the seedlings appeared, we had to hill up dirt around them. And throughout the growing season, we had to hoe the weeds at least once a week.

This was evening work—especially during the school year. In the still air, clouds of biting sand gnats attacked our faces, hair, wrists, ankles, and ears—any part of us they could get to. Sometimes mosquitoes joined them. When the bugs were really bad, Pop would have us make up a "smoke pot" with some of Momma's old rags and dried manure. The stinking smoke would drive off the bugs—and us, if we'd had the choice.

We were organic gardeners before organic was cool. Manure, ashes from the woodstove, and dishwater (we used Octagon soap) were our only fertilizers. We picked bugs off the plants with our hands, and if the bean beetles got bad, Momma would sprinkle ashes from the woodstove on the plants to drive them away. I don't remember ever watering our crops. It seemed our rain was more regular then than it is these days. We took care to plant crops that needed a lot of water in low places and others that might rot, such as melons, on higher ground.

Momma and Pop knew when it was time to pick everything, from beans to watermelon. Pop would wrap his hand around a brown-tasseled ear of corn to gauge when the kernels were full and even along the ears. He prided himself on judging watermelons and cantaloupes with a solid thump of his finger. "Disyah one ready," he'd say. "But dis one need some mo' time."

Picking pole beans in the garden.

Momma didn't like dirty clothes or dirt in her house. And I remember summer evenings when we would have to hose each other off or bathe outside in the washtub before we could come in.

But when it came to gardening, we were allowed to get dirty. You'd think that would make gardening fun, but we learned quickly the difference between work and play. We could change games when we wanted, but work had to be done regardless of our mood.

 BLACK-EYED PEA SOUP

1 pound dried black-eyed peas (any field peas or cowpeas will do)
3 pieces smoked pork neck bone
3 pieces fresh pig tail
3 pieces Joe Louis strip or ham hocks
1 fresh pig's foot, split
1 small onion, chopped
salt and black pepper to taste

Empty the peas into a bowl, pick out any bad ones, add water, and soak for 30 to 60 minutes. Wash all the meat well and boil in a medium-large pot for 20 to 30 minutes, then drain. Leaving the meat inside, refill the pot two-thirds full with water and bring to a boil again. Drain the peas and wash again. Add the peas and onion to the meat in the pot. Cook until peas are tender (1 to 2 hours), taste, then add salt and pepper as desired. Serve in a bowl, over rice or grits.

COUNTRY-FRIED CABBAGE WITH HAM

1 medium head cabbage
2 tablespoons oil
1 pound cooked ham, sliced about 1/8 inch thick
1 onion, cut into wedges
salt and black pepper to taste

Peel off the outer layer of the cabbage and throw it away. Cut the cabbage into quarters, then halve the quarters again (I cut mine up even more), wash, and drain thoroughly. Heat the oil in a medium pot, fry the ham slices on both sides for a minute or two, until browned, and remove from the oil. Lower the heat, allowing the oil to cool some before adding the drained cabbage and onion. Stir-fry the cabbage and onion over medium heat until they're as tender you like (some folks prefer their cabbage and onions fairly crisp), add the ham, then the salt and pepper. Serve the cabbage on its own or over rice, and enjoy.

MOMMA'S HOMEGROWN COLLARDS

Nutritionists call collards a perfect food, offering nearly everything you need to survive. While they're easy to grow year-round in Daufuskie's climate, winter collards are sweeter and more tender. Besides, they were the only thing, other than turnips and rutabagas, in our winter garden.

Momma called them "greens fo' da soul." She would cook up a batch for nearly every Sunday dinner—with fried chicken, red rice, and tada salad. Church was at noon and dinner followed at 2:00 or 3:00. If Momma didn't go to church, she'd be finishing the meal when we walked in the door. If Momma did go, she'd get up early and cook, then have dinner waiting on the back burner. As we walked into the yard, the simmering collards would greet us with their distinct aroma. We couldn't change out of our Sunday clothes fast enough to sit down to Momma's collards (not to mention the rest of the meal).

1 large bunch collards (about a third of a bushel basket if you pick your own)
2 pieces smoked pork neck bone
2–3 pieces fresh pig tail
½ fresh pig's foot
1 ham hock
1 large onion, diced
salt and black pepper to taste

Cut the collards into 1- to 2-inch pieces, wash them in warm to hot water at least two or three times, then leave them in warm water until needed. Place all the meat in a large pot, two-thirds filled with water, cover, then boil 20 to 30 minutes. Drain the water and refill the pot, then cover and boil the meat again for about an hour. Drain the collards, add them to the cooked meat and stock, along with the onion, salt, and pepper. Cook the whole potful for another 30 to 45 minutes. Some people like greens cooked less, so they're chewy. The longer you cook them, the tenderer they get. Serve alone, over rice, grits, or potatoes, or as a side dish.

YELLOW SQUASH WITH BACON

5–6 large (or 10–12 small) yellow summer squash
3 strips bacon
1 medium onion, chopped
½ cup hot water
salt and black pepper to taste

Wash the squash well, then cut crossways into quarter-inch-thick round pieces. Fry the bacon strips in a skillet, then remove, leaving the grease. Add the squash and onion to the grease and stir-fry over medium heat until they start to brown. Add the bacon strips and hot water, then salt and pepper to taste as the mixture simmers 10 to 15 minutes. Serve as a side dish with whatever you like.

SEA ISLAND OKRA GUMBO

Momma says she'll never forget the day I was born. As she was entering her ninth month with me, living in Savannah, she decided to take a pregnancy leave from work, thinking she had enough time to go to Daufuskie and visit her parents, who needed help with some work around the house.

Several days into her visit, on August 4, she recalls feeling pretty good as she went into the yard to scrub some clothes on a washboard in a tub. As she worked, a pot of okra gumbo cooked slowly on the woodstove in the kitchen. Momma says she spent half the day scrubbing clothes and grew hungry from smelling the long pot's 'roma.

By the time she finished with the wash, all she wanted to do was eat. She was just stepping into the kitchen to prepare her meal, when, suddenly, she felt a great pain. She couldn't bear it long enough to eat even a bite. Into the bedroom she went, and off ran Grandmomma, through a shortcut in the woods. She rushed past her big field of okra, danced across the board that bridged a shallow pond, and hurried down the path on the other side—yelling the whole way—to fetch the island midwife.

It wasn't long before I arrived. Momma says she was hungry and tired. But I was crying for something to eat, so she breast-fed me right away. She was not allowed to eat her okra gumbo, because it had fresh pork in it. (My Grandmomma had a strict rule that women who had just given birth could not eat fresh meat for a month.) Momma says the only thing she was given to eat that evening was soda crackers and water.

"Back in dem ol' days, de ol' folks always had sumptin' you couldn' eat when ya wanted to," Momma says. "'Specially after you just had a baby."

Regardless, to this day I do not eat okra and don't even like the smell of it. But Grandmomma was always proud of her rows of chest-high okra plants, and no Daufuskie cookbook would be complete without Momma's gumbo.

2 pieces ham hock
3 pieces fresh pig tail
1–2 cans diced or stewed tomatoes
4–5 cups water
3 cups okra, cut up
1 cup shrimp, peeled and deveined
corn, green beans (optional)

Put the pig tail and ham hock in a medium pot, half full with water. Boil 20 minutes, then drain. This will clean the meat. Rinse the meat again, twice. Return the meat to the pot, add the tomatoes (more or less, as you prefer) and 4 to 5 cups of water, and boil slowly until the meat is tender and tomatoes break down in the soup (30 to 60 minutes). If you wish, prefry the okra with a dash of oil to reduce the slime. Add the okra, prefried or not, along with shrimp, to the tomatoes and meat. If you like, add corn, green beans, or any other vegetable, canned or fresh. Cook for another 20 to 30 minutes over medium heat. Serve as a soup, over rice, or with stiff grits.

HAM HOCKS AND RUTABAGAS

1–2 medium rutabagas
2 ham hocks, split in half
1 small onion, diced
salt and black pepper to taste

Rutabaga is a very tasty vegetable if prepared and cooked right. The trick is to completely peel and dice the round, hard roots and rinse the pieces thoroughly. Set the diced rutabaga aside in a bowl of water. Place the ham hocks in a medium pot, two-thirds filled with warm water, and boil for 15 minutes. Drain and refill the pot with warm water, then boil the ham hocks again until half cooked—when you can just stick a fork through the tough skin, which usually takes 1 to 2 hours, depending on the size of the hocks. Drain the pot again and refill to the two-thirds level with warm water. Add the onion and rutabaga pieces, and boil again. Cook over medium-high heat, stirring occasionally, 30 to 45 minutes. When the rutabaga is tender, the ham hocks will be fully cooked. Add salt and pepper to taste. You can mash the rutabaga or leave it as is. Dig in with a fork for a wonderful taste that will surprise you.

SMOKIN' JOE BUTTER BEANS

For some reason, most folks called my grandmother "Blossom." But my sisters and I don't remember her as flowery. She was a big woman who filled a room with her voice. Although she clearly loved all her 44 grandchildren, she wasn't about to repeat things she told us to do—or not do.

If she had any soft spots, they were her vegetable garden and her kitchen. When she was in either place, we would never think of entering without asking her permission. This was tough on us when it was cold, because the kitchen was the warmest spot in the house. Grandmomma's woodstove sat along its back wall, where blackened pans and pots hung from nails pounded into the pine planks. Ten minutes beside the stove could take off the coldest winter chill. And on hot days, we sought out the bucket of pumped water on a stand in the corner. A lid kept dirt and bugs out, and a dipper sat beside it. We scooped our own water with that dipper, but unless we wanted to get popped in the mouth, we didn't drink from the dipper. That's what tin cups were for.

Grandmomma grew most all the vegetables she cooked, including her famous butter (lima) beans. In season, she would sit on the porch, her big apron spread across her open legs as a work area, shelling the beans into a pan. If we were nearby, she'd hand each of us a pan so we could work beside her. She lay the shelled beans in the sun on a croaker (burlap) sack, set atop an old sheet of hot tin roofing. Every few hours, two of us would grab either end of the croaker sack and toss the beans in the air, to turn and dry them evenly.

The dried beans cooked—whether the next day or the next year—in a "long pot." Shortly after breakfast, Grandmomma would fill the pot and set it on the woodstove. Throughout the day, while we worked on chores in the yard, it simmered, spreading its aroma so we could hardly resist a taste.

It seemed the sweet smell would overwhelm us about the time "Love of Life" came on Grandmomma's old black-and-white television. But we didn't dare ask when we could eat, because interrupting her soap opera was almost as bad as being caught playing in her garden.

3 pieces smoked pork neck bone (or Joe Louis strip)
3 pieces fresh pig tail
2 pieces ham hocks
2 cups dried or fresh butter (lima) beans
salt and black pepper to taste

Place the meat in a medium-large pot, about two-thirds full with water, boil 30 minutes, then drain. Rinse the meat thoroughly and place it back in pot, again two-thirds filled with fresh water. Empty the lima beans into a bowl and pick out any bad ones. Rinse them several times in water and add to the pot with the meat. Add salt and pepper to taste. Boil gently over medium heat until the beans are tender—or at least 2 hours, to make sure the meat cooks thoroughly. If cooking with fresh limas, don't add the beans until the meat has cooked on its own for at least 1 hour. Serve with rice or alone for good, basic eating.

SNAP BEANS WITH TADAS

2 pieces fatback bacon
2 pieces fresh pig tail
3 pieces smoked pork neck bone
1½ pounds snap (string or green) beans
5–6 medium potatoes, cut in half
salt and black pepper to taste

Fry the fatback and set aside. Place the pig tail and neck bone in a medium pot, half filled with warm water, and boil 20 to 30 minutes. While the meat boils, snap and wash the beans, then wash and cut the potatoes. Add the beans to the pot and cook 20 minutes; then add the potatoes, fatback, and (if needed) a cup or so of hot water. Cook until the potatoes are as tender as you like. Add salt and pepper to taste. Serve as a side dish or over rice as a meal.

TURNIPS AND GREENS

3 pieces smoked pork neck bone
2 pieces fresh pork neck bone
1 ham hock, split in half
1 bunch turnip greens, with 4–5 turnip bottoms
1 medium onion, cut into wedges
salt and black pepper to taste

Wash all the meat thoroughly. Place it in a large pot, two-thirds filled with water, and boil 20 to 30 minutes. As the meat cooks, cut turnips from the greens, peel, and dice. Pick the stems from the greens and cut into 2- to 3-inch pieces. Wash and drain the greens and turnips 2 or 3 times in cool water. Drain the water from the meat in the pot, refill halfway with fresh hot water, and boil again. Add the turnips and onion to the pot and boil 30 minutes or longer. Add the greens and boil until they're as tender as you like them. Add salt and pepper to taste. Serve as a side dish or over rice for a meal.

GULLAH-FRIED SWEET TADAS

Sweet potatoes were introduced to European culture by Christopher Columbus, who found them cultivated on the Caribbean island of St. Thomas. Often called yams, they are not even related to those much-larger, sweeter, and darker tubers that grow in Latin America—nor are they related to white potatoes. But for early South Carolina settlers and in slave times, sweet potatoes were a staple.

Rich in vitamin A, potassium, and other nutrients, with no fat, sweet potatoes make good energy food. Field workers and hunters carried baked "sweet tadas"—with their skins serving as a natural wrapper—in their pockets or aprons for a midday meal. Even when I was a child on Daufuskie, our winter lunches often were just a baked sweet potato and a piece of fried fish in a brown paper bag—which was a real belly full.

Grandmomma always grew a big field of sweet potato vines. When we dug the sweet potatoes right after the first frost in the late fall, we separated out the small tubers for seed to be planted in the spring and "banked" both them and the eating sweet potatoes in a special, tin-roofed, A-frame shed. Sweet potatoes don't keep well in a refrigerator or at room temperature, and when any part of one rots, the flavor of the whole tuber is spoiled. The banking kept them cool, but not cold, moist but not wet, and away from varmints. First, we dug a hole in the dirt floor of the shed, then we put down a thick layer of pine straw in the bottom of the hole. The sweet potatoes went on top of the pine straw, and they were topped with another layer of pine straw. Finally, we piled a mound of dirt over the hole.

This way, we stored our crop all winter and well into spring, when we dug out the seed and laid them tip-to-tip in trenches dug in mounded garden rows. After about a month, each seed potato would sprout several vines. We cut those vines, which were already sprouting roots, at ground level, then transplanted them into 6-inch-high, moist hills to raise the next fall's crop.

We grew orange sweet potatoes, but there are also yellow varieties, which aren't quite as sweet or moist, and many folks consider them a delicacy. I use the former in this recipe and in my sweet tada bread and pone, but yellow ones would work, too.

This is a simple recipe, just one step beyond tossing a sweet tada in the oven or on the coals. But it's always a hit.

4–5 sweet potatoes
1 cup cooking oil
salt (optional)

Wash and peel the sweet potatoes, then slice them crossways or diagonally into quarter-inch-thick pieces. Heat the oil in a skillet. Place the potato slices in the hot oil and cook until browned on both sides and tender. Place the cooked slices on a napkin or paper towel to drain the oil. Sprinkle with salt, if desired, and serve them any way you like, as a side dish or even an appetizer.

BOILED PEANUTS

I often think no truly Southern garden is complete without peanuts. They grow quickly and easily, and they add nitrogen to the soil, protein to the diet, and fun for the children, who always enjoy digging in the dirt to find the peanuts left behind when you pull up the blooming plants.

We always grew plenty of the root crop that European settlers found when they came to America. And our crop was a snack that Momma and Pop always let us have. We dried much of the crop, saving them for winter munching—either raw or roasted in the oven. But the rest we boiled "green," fresh from the warm, summer soil. We cooked them outside in a big pot of salty water, over a slow fire in the August heat.

Throughout the Deep South, signs on the roadside and in convenience store windows advertise fresh boiled peanuts. In most of the rest of the country, peanuts are something you grind up and spread on bread with jelly, eat at the ball game, or gobble, roasted and salted, from a can or jar. But to many Southern folks, boiled peanuts are the best snack around.

2 pounds green peanuts in shells (look in the produce section in late summer)
½ cup salt
6–8 quarts water

Wash the peanuts thoroughly in hot water (remember, they came right out of the dirt). Dissolve the salt in a big stew pot, three-quarters full with water. Add the washed peanuts, still in their shells, and boil until done. That can be 1 to 3 hours, depending on how fresh the peanuts are and how soft you like them. Sample often (children are always eager to help). Once the peanuts are cooked to your liking, allow them to sit in the water as it cools for 30 minutes or longer to absorb the salty flavor. Serve hot or cold in a bowl or bag, with the beverage of your choice and a good ball game or sunset to watch as you shell and eat them.

The River

Daufuskie was and remains very much an island. It has no bridge and only limited public ferries from the mainland. Surrounded by deep water and wide marshes, we had to make the best of our situation.

And when you get right down to it, our situation wasn't so bad. The tidal waters around Daufuskie are filled with seafood. The nearby May River and New River marshes are among the most productive in the United States. However, there was a problem with these waters: the Savannah River, as it emptied into the Atlantic just over a mile to our south, carried pollution from industrial plants upriver. This pollution cost Daufuskie our only industry, a world-famous oyster cannery, which public health officials shut down in the 1950s.

Without the jobs associated with the cannery, many islanders left. Nevertheless, when I was coming up in the 1960s, those of us still living on Daufuskie learned to find safe, tasty meals from the waters around us and cook them up to perfection.

As with most foods we gathered and caught, there was a time for every species in the "river," as Pop referred to all the waters—sound, ocean, creek, or river—around Daufuskie. Even in January, folks with warm clothes, good reflexes, and a bucket of tiny fiddler crabs for bait could catch sheepshead around the pilings of docks. And off and on through the cooler months, when the water was clear, the speckled sea trout would run, offering some of the most exciting fishing you could find. Mild, tasty whiting, hard-fighting spottail bass (red drum), and yellowtails showed up in the spring, then returned, like the trout, each fall. During the hottest months, we would fish on the bottom for sea bass, croaker, catfish, and, if we were really lucky, flounder.

From fall to early summer, we cast our nets over deep holes in the creeks. We'd haul them in, heavy with mullet. We'd cast for shrimp starting in midsummer, and by fall, they'd be big and plentiful.

Pop made all our cast nets. He'd sit on the porch for days in the summer knitting nets, and in the winter he'd park by the wood heater in the living room. He'd carve his 8- to 10-inch-long needles from hardwood and use a flat wooden spacer—thicker for mullet nets, thinner for shrimp—to guide his knitting of cotton or nylon twine. "Bring dat spool o' yarn yah," he'd call to us. Then he would focus on the work, sitting and talking for hours with anyone who would join him.

And he taught all of us girls how to both knit and throw the nets. We giggled in the yard as he showed us how to hold in our mouths one of the sinkers that circle a net, then release it as we spread the net.

From spring through fall, shrimp trawlers would pull in at the public dock. Many captains and mates aboard the boats, which often spent days at sea, were related to islanders and generous to us. From them, we'd buy the deepwater catch of shark, scallops, squid, and exotic fish, along with crabs and, of course, shrimp. What didn't end up in the frying pan usually found its way into the stew pot.

From about Easter to Thanksgiving, when the water was warm enough to get the blue crabs moving, we crabbed—with hand lines and nets, and with a wire trap we'd dangle from an old dock.

Despite the pollution that shut down the oyster factory, old-time islanders knew areas nearby where it was safe to gather shellfish in the cooler months. As children, we joined in to dig for conchs (actually whelks) and clams on the beach. Adults took on the heavy, rather dangerous work of picking razor-sharp oysters from shell banks in the soft marsh mud.

As with the gathering, preparing most seafood was a family affair. We headed and peeled shrimp, cooked and picked crab, cleaned and scaled fish, cracked and shucked shellfish together.

It was work. But I remember, as a child, it was also fun. We learned the ways of God's creatures. We appreciated where our favorite foods came from.

And we ate well.

BROKEN CRAB AND OKRA STEW

4–6 raw blue crabs
2–3 fatback bacon strips
1 medium onion, cut into wedges
1½ cups water
1 can stewed tomatoes (optional)
salt and black pepper to taste
2 cups cut okra

Pour boiling water on the crabs to stun them so you won't get pinched. "Debark" and clean them (remove the top shell and gills), break them in half, and, if desired, remove their legs and back fins. Fry the bacon in a large skillet, then add the crab pieces, onion, water, and if desired, stewed tomatoes. Add salt and pepper to taste and simmer 15 minutes; add the okra and boil gently, stirring often, 15 to 20 minutes—or simmer until the okra is tender but the crab is still firm. Serve alone, with cornbread, or over rice or grits. And use your fingers to pick up shell pieces and suck out the sweet crabmeat.

 'FUSKIE CRAB PATTIES

HOW TO PICK CRABS

Before you can pick a crab, you have to cook it. Boil or steam live blue crabs in a large pot for about 10 minutes or longer, which turns them from blue to deep red. We used a little salt in the boiling water. Some folks add all kinds of spices, even beer, but if you're picking the crab for meat to use in a recipe, it doesn't make much difference.

Every crab lover has his or her own way of picking crabs, but many of those methods either take lots of time or leave a lot of crabmeat behind. To get the most crab from the shell in the least amount of time, on 'Fuskie we worked with sharp paring knives. First, we removed the "bark," or top shell (saving it, intact, for our deviled crabs, which we sold to tourists), and the lungs, or "dead men." We left the yellow fat, but many folks take it out. Then we would rinse the crabs, break them in half, and remove the legs, back fins, and claws.

Next, we cut the halves into two pieces each. This opened up the chambers formed by the legs in the shell. Being careful not to cut ourselves with the knives or sharp shells, we worked our knife points between the meat and the shell pieces and then used the knife to pull out the crab in chunks. We did this with each chamber in the shells. Adults in our house worked on the lump meat, while the children cracked the claws. We would hit them hard—but not so hard that we would crush the shell into the meat—with the heavy handle of a knife (although many folks use nutcrackers instead). Usually, we just tossed out the legs and back fins, but you can bite or break the ends off and squeeze meat from them if you want to.

Pop was the crab pickin' expert. He would call my sisters and me in from playing in the yard, then supervise the operation on the front porch. "Y'all bark dem crabs," he'd command. "Gitcha some bowls and butter knife [he wouldn't let his little girls use sharp knives], den crack and pick dem claws, while Bertha [that is, Momma] and me pick da rest."

2 cups crabmeat (lump and claw)
1 medium onion, diced
½ medium green bell pepper, diced
½ medium red bell pepper, diced
2 eggs, beaten
1 tablespoon flour
½ teaspoon salt
½ teaspoon black pepper
¾ cup cooking oil or bacon grease

Now that you've worked hard picking the crabs, it's time to make something tasty out of them. Thoroughly combine all of the ingredients except the oil and form the mixture into patties. Heat the oil in a skillet, then fry the patties, turning once, until brown on both sides. Serve on their own, as a main dish with rice or grits, in a sandwich, or however you like.

A blue crab, fresh from the water.

SCOOP NET FRIED CRAB

¼ cup cooking oil or bacon grease
1 medium onion, chopped
1 medium green bell pepper, chopped
1 stalk celery, chopped
2 cups crabmeat (lump and claw)
salt and black pepper to taste

Heat the oil in a skillet. Brown the onions, bell pepper, and celery, then add the crabmeat and stir-fry until the crab is brown. Add salt and pepper to taste. Serve over rice or grits, with fresh cornbread on the side.

FRIED CRAB STEW

This recipe is an old favorite, very similar to scoop net fried crab, but with water, bacon, and some extra cooking added.

3 strips bacon
2 cups crabmeat (lump and claw)
1 medium onion, chopped
1 medium green bell pepper, chopped
1 stalk celery, chopped
½ cup hot water
salt and black pepper to taste

Fry the bacon in a skillet. In a bowl, combine the crabmeat, onion, bell pepper, and celery. Set the bacon aside and fry the crab and vegetable mixture in the drippings in the skillet, stirring often, until the crab begins to brown. Crumble the bacon and add to the skillet, along with ½ cup hot water. Cover and simmer 15 to 20 minutes. Stir often. Add salt and pepper to taste. Serve over rice, grits, or biscuits.

POPPIN' FRIED SHRIMP

2 cups shrimp, peeled and deveined
1 cup flour
sprinkle salt and black pepper
sprinkle paprika
sprinkle garlic powder
1 cup (or more) cooking oil

Season the shrimp with the salt, pepper, paprika, and garlic powder, put them in a bag with the flour, and shake to coat well. Shake excess flour from the shrimp and place them in a skillet with a half inch of hot oil. (Test the oil temperature by dropping in a dab of flour; adjust the heat so the flour browns, not burns.) Fry until golden brown on both sides. Don't overcook them, or the shrimp will be too chewy to enjoy. Go ahead and eat 'em up with your fingers. It's OK.

Note: For battered shrimp, mix 1 cup milk and 2 beaten eggs, and dip the seasoned shrimp in the mixture before coating with flour.

Sallie casts for shrimp as Pop taught her.

COOPER RIVER SMUTTERED SHRIMP

1 cup cooking oil or bacon grease
2 cups shrimp, peeled and deveined
sprinkle paprika
sprinkle salt and black pepper
sprinkle garlic powder
1 cup flour
1 medium onion, chopped
½ medium green bell pepper, chopped
1 stalk celery, chopped
2 cups hot water

Heat the oil in a skillet. Sprinkle the shrimp with paprika, salt, pepper, and garlic powder. Place the flour in a bag or bowl, add the seasoned shrimp, and shake or toss to coat well. Test the oil temperature by dropping in a dab of flour and adjust the heat so the flour browns, not burns. Shake excess flour from the shrimp, then add them to the hot skillet and cook until brown on both sides (don't overcook or the shrimp will get chewy). Drain the oil. Add the onion, bell pepper, celery, and hot water. Add more seasoning, if needed, to taste. Cover the skillet and simmer 10 to 15 minutes, until the gravy thickens. Serve over rice, grits, or potatoes.

DAUFUSKIE CATFISH AND SHRIMP MULL

2 pieces fatback bacon
4–6 saltwater catfish (gutted, with skins on—catfish have no scales)
1 cup shrimp, peeled and deveined
1 medium onion, chopped

½ medium green bell pepper, chopped
1 scallion or green onion, sliced
1½ cups warm water
salt and black pepper to taste

In a skillet, fry the fatback. When done, set the fatback aside, leaving excess grease in the skillet on medium heat. Wash the catfish and shrimp. Place the catfish in the skillet and fry 2 to 4 minutes, until brown on one side. Add the shrimp on top of the catfish, along with the onion, bell pepper, scallion, and cooked bacon. Add the water and salt and pepper to taste, cover the skillet, and cook 15 to 25 minutes over low heat until a thin gravy forms. Serve over rice or grits for a real knockout dish. Watch for catfish bones as you eat.

FRIED SHARK

8–10 shark steak pieces (1–1½ pounds total)
sprinkle salt and black pepper
sprinkle garlic powder
sprinkle paprika
½ cup flour
½ cup vegetable oil or bacon grease

Sprinkle the shark pieces with salt, pepper, garlic powder, and paprika, then coat with flour. In a skillet, heat the oil (test the oil temperature by dropping in a dab of flour and adjust the heat so the flour browns, not burns) and fry, turning occasionally, until golden brown.

DOCKSIDE BAKED SHEEPSHEAD

Sheepshead are fairly large, flat, crafty fish with vertical stripes and tough mouths filled with sharp teeth. They live near dock pilings or submerged debris, where they find their food—barnacles and small shellfish, including fiddler crabs. We caught sheepshead in cool weather, when the water was clear, by dangling fiddler crabs on sharp hooks beside the dock pilings.

Pop and Momma knew just the right time and tide for sheepshead fishing. And when that time was near, they would send my sisters and me to the nearby marsh, where we would round up the fiddlers. We knew where the mud was firm and the 1-inch (and smaller) crabs guarded their holes. The males each have one large claw for attracting females and defending their territory. We didn't care. We snuck up on them, chased them so fast that they'd run right past their holes, and then scooped them up in our bare hands. Fairly often, they pinched us, but it didn't hurt much. Within a short time, the three of us would cover the bottom of a bucket with skittering, little crabs.

Some days, Pop and Momma used fishing rods, other days cane poles or even drop lines. Each of them would carefully hook a crab through its belly and dangle it beside what they figured was the best dock piling for catching fish. Pop made my sisters and me sit still or go up on the hill, because "all dat racket y'all chillen makin' is gonna scare off da big fish." And that's what they were after. Sometimes they would need to halve the fish to fit it in the roaster pan.

My parents loved each other, but they both had competitive streaks. And sheepshead are hard to catch: they can suck the bait right off a hook, and you need to strike back hard to set your hook in their tough mouths. If Momma caught the biggest fish, Pop would be days livin' it down. If he caught the biggest fish, Momma would hear about it for months.

"Bertha," he'd say, "ya ain't no fishaman. Ya is a woman. And da fish be smart 'nuff he ain't gonna git caught on no woman's line." Momma never answered Pop when he talked that way. She'd just go catch a bigger fish and smile as she served it to him.

This recipe is good for just about any baked fish, but there's none much better than sheepshead.

2–3 medium, or 1–2 large, sheepshead
sprinkle salt and black pepper
sprinkle garlic powder
1 medium onion, cut into wedges
1 medium green bell pepper, chopped
1 cup water
fresh lemon slices for garnish (optional)

Scale and gut the fish (my parents left the heads on). Wash the fish thoroughly, pat dry, then sprinkle with salt, pepper, and garlic powder, inside and out. Lay the fish in opposite directions in a greased baking pan, to help them cook evenly. Spread the onion and bell pepper over and around the fish, then add water, cover with foil, and bake in a preheated oven at 350° for 20 to 30 minutes. The aroma of the fish will let you know when it's ready to eat. Serve with rice or grits and use the pan drippings as a gravy.

POP'S SMUTTERED MULLET (WITH STIFF GRITS)

Pop loved fish. And he loved fishing. Momma called him a porpoise, because he could catch and eat as much as the bottle-nosed dolphins that rule the creeks around Daufuskie.

He seldom tired of throwing a cast net for mullet and never tired of eating them. Still, much as he loved his fish, he was generous, usually sharing his catch with other islanders.

When the big-eyed, bullet-shaped mullet were running in the creeks, Pop would cast—if he could—on every dropping tide. He knew every deep hole around the island. And sometimes on warmer days, he'd make us stand in knee-deep water at the mouth of a creek to scare the schools of fish back into his "mullet hole." The water would boil around us with jumping mullet, many over a foot long, and Pop's net would be heavy with flopping fish.

Smuttered mullet—over grits or rice, or just plain—was Pop's favorite meal. He could, and sometimes did, eat it three times a day. When Momma couldn't or wouldn't cook it, he'd do it himself, simmering the whole fish in bacon grease and water. Stiff grits—cooked thicker than normal—are probably the best base for the stewed fish and gravy.

As children, sometimes we'd complain about eating so much fish. But Pop would shut us up. "Grits is grocery," he'd say. "An' a mess o' fish wit' grits fills da belly."

3–4 strips bacon
4–6 medium-to-large mullet, cleaned and scaled
sprinkle salt and black pepper
1 medium onion, chopped (or 2 green onion tops, sliced)
1 cup hot water
1 cup dry grits cooked with about 2½ cups water

Put the bacon in a pan and fry until crisp. Remove the bacon but leave the grease in the pan. Sprinkle the fish lightly with salt and pepper, and add to the pan. Fry the fish 3 to 5 minutes without turning, then add the onion and water. Lay the bacon over the fish, add more salt and pepper to taste, cover, and simmer 10 to 15 minutes. Cook the grits in a separate pot, adding a sprinkle of salt. Serve the fish and golden pan juices over the grits and no one will leave the table hungry.

BENJIE'S POINT STEWED CROAKER

3 strips bacon
4–5 medium croaker or similar fish, scaled and cleaned
sprinkle salt and black pepper
1 medium onion, diced
1 small green bell pepper, diced
1½ cups hot water

Fry the bacon in a skillet until crisp. Remove the bacon but leave the grease in the skillet. Sprinkle salt and pepper over and inside the croaker, then add them to the hot grease in the skillet. Fry over medium-high heat 2 to 4 minutes, until lightly browned on one side. Add the bacon, onion, bell pepper, and water to the skillet. Cover and simmer 15 to 20 minutes, until the fish is tender. Serve over rice or stiff grits.

SKILLET-FRIED TROUT

No fish was prized more on Daufuskie than speckled sea trout. As the days shortened and the water chilled, the hard-fighting, tasty-eating fish would swim up into the creeks and marshes around the island.

Most folks on the island didn't have boats, so we would stake our spots on the shore, often around old dock pilings, and cast our lines baited with shrimp. I can remember watching every twitch of the line as the sun

Casting a fishing line for trout at a public dock.

set and the tide rose. Someone down the bank would call out, "I got one!" Then, "Oh goodness! Disyah feels like a real big'un!"

Well, maybe it was, maybe it wasn't. Because even a little trout puts up a big fight. Nevertheless, everyone would turn to look and congratulate the fisherman (or -woman). But you can bet we were all thinking about how we'd catch a bigger fish in a few minutes.

As it got dark, we would pack up our rods and compare our catch. The person with the biggest fish could brag until the next day. But what we really cared about was suppertime.

2–4 trout, cleaned and scaled
sprinkle salt and black pepper
1 cup flour
1 cup cooking oil or bacon grease

After cleaning and rinsing the fish, pat them dry with a paper towel, and then sprinkle them inside and out with salt and pepper. Put the flour in a bag (paper or plastic), add the fish, and shake until fully coated. Heat the oil in a skillet, testing the oil temperature by dropping in a dab of flour and adjusting the heat so the flour browns, not burns. Shake excess flour from the fish and add them to the hot oil in the skillet. Cook them for several minutes to brown one side, then turn. After you brown both sides, the fish are ready for some fine eating—although some folks (like me) like to fry their fish a little longer, until they're nice and crispy.

FRIED WHITING

As summer approached, whiting would begin feeding below docks and beside pilings on Daufuskie, and we'd begin fishing for them. You can buy farm-raised whiting, as well as saltwater whiting, in many good grocery stores and fish markets. But if you have a choice, pick the tastier saltwater fish.

4–6 whiting (or other mild fish), cleaned and scaled, and filleted, if you like
sprinkle salt and black pepper
sprinkle paprika
1 cup cooking oil
1 cup flour, cornmeal, or a combination of the two

Wash the fish and pat dry, laying them on a flat surface and sprinkling them with salt, pepper, and paprika on both sides. Heat the oil in a medium skillet until it is hot enough to brown, but not burn, a dab of flour dropped into it. Place the flour and/or cornmeal in a plastic or paper bag. Add 2 or 3 fish, hold the top of the bag closed tightly, and shake the bag until the fish are well coated. Repeat until all of the fish are coated. Shake off excess flour and/or meal and set each fish in the hot oil to fry, turning after several minutes to evenly brown each side. Remove the fish from the oil and lay on a paper towel atop a pan or plate to drain the excess grease. Serve with rice, grits, potatoes, or cornbread.

CONCH SOUP (WITH SMOKED NECK BONE)

Conchs and whelks are really just large seagoing snails. We used to gather whelks (which we called "conchs") on the Bloody Point beach at Daufuskie's south end. They would be buried in the muddy areas, with just the tips of their shells showing at low tide. If you didn't know what you were looking for, you wouldn't notice them.

Sometimes the mud was so soft it could grab you and swallow you, like quicksand. I remember one or two Jeeps getting stuck in the mud and sinking. If folks went digging today, they might just find a windshield or a tire down deep. But as they dug, they'd almost certainly find a few conchs.

My family would go conch digging in the early fall, when the water was still warm and we could wade barefoot along the shore. My sisters and I would hitch Bobby the cow to his cart, load it with pick rakes, buckets, and croaker sacks (burlap bags), and roll down Beach Road. At the beach, we'd split up in pairs and search sections of the shore. When one of us spotted a conch, we'd scream, "Find one!" We'd race each other to the shell tip and dig out the conch. Then we'd feel around with our fingers in the sticky mud, or rake the area, and usually find a few more.

We would fill our buckets and bags until they were so heavy we had to drag them and get Pop to help us load them into the wagon. Then we would head back home.

Once or twice each year, we built a big fire right on the beach, roasted the conchs in their shells, and then pulled the chewy meat out with a fork and ate it. But most times, we brought the catch home, where we either parboiled the conchs and pulled the meat out or cracked the shells with hammers. While we girls tapped away with hammers, Momma or Pop would crack twice as many with the back of our ax. Conch was special for us, and we all loved the fun of gathering and fixing it, as well as eating it.

Roasted conch is so chewy that we could eat only one or two. The rest Momma cooked up some other way, and one of her favorite recipes was for conch soup.

4 pieces smoked pork neck bone
3 strips bacon
1 medium onion, chopped
1 medium green bell pepper, chopped
2 tablespoons flour
1 tablespoon cooking oil
8–10 shelled conch, cut into bite-size pieces
salt and black pepper to taste

Half fill a pot with water, add the neck bone, and boil about 30 minutes. Drain and refill the pot halfway, then boil the neck bone again over medium heat as you prepare the other ingredients. Fry the bacon in a skillet; when it's done, remove the bacon and leave the grease in the skillet. Lightly stir-fry the onion and bell pepper in the grease, then remove them and add to the pot with the neck bone. Add the flour and oil to the grease in the skillet, stirring the mixture constantly over medium heat as the flour browns and a paste forms. Add the flour mixture to the boiling pot with the neck bone and vegetables, and stir well. Stir in the conch. Crumble the cooked bacon and add to the pot. Continuc to boil an hour or more, stirring occasionally, until the conch is tender in a medium-thick gravy. Add more water if needed, and salt and pepper to taste. Serve as soup in a bowl, over grits, or with rice.

SHUCKIN' FRIED OYSTERS

For years, picking and shucking oysters formed the basis of the Daufuskie economy. My great-grandparents and grandparents, as well as many people of my parents' generation, were skilled workers at the old concrete-block oyster factory on the island's south end. Oyster shells paved our roads and reinforced our boat landing against erosion.

Oystermen and -women worked during the cooler months—those with an "r" in their names—under layers of clothes, their hands covered in old socks to protect them from the cold and the sharp shells. Chatting in quick Gullah phrases and chewing snuff, they worked along tables that ran nearly the length of the building. The men would gather the oysters, walking through mud at low tide and loading their catch into flat-bottomed bateaus, powered by oars. As they returned on the rising tide, they would wash the oysters and shovel them onto the tables for the women to shuck. The women slipped sturdy knifes into tight shells and scooped the sweet contents into buckets. The men shoveled away piles of shells, replacing them with freshly gathered oysters.

My parents never worked at the factory, which was failing by the early 1950s, as pollution from the growing industrial port of Savannah spread to many of the oyster beds around Daufuskie. As children, we played in the abandoned building and watched unemployed neighbors move away, across the water.

But islanders who stayed knew where the oysters were still safe, and during the winter they were basic food for us. The community gathered for roasts, where we laid a sheet of steel over a hot fire, then topped it with oysters covered by wet croaker (burlap) sacks. And for a special treat, Momma would roll the juicy oysters in flour and fry them up.

Opening an oyster.

1 quart shucked oysters
sprinkle salt and black pepper
1 cup self-rising flour
1½ cups vegetable oil

Wash and drain the oysters. Season them with salt and pepper while the oil is heating in a deep skillet. Coat the oysters in flour, shake off the excess, then set them in the hot oil. (Test the oil temperature by dropping in a dab of flour and adjust the heat so the flour browns, not burns.) Fry until golden brown. Don't overcook them or oysters get chewy.

Note: We fried our oysters with just flour for coating, but many folks these days prefer to dip their washed oysters in a mixture of 1 cup milk and 2 beaten eggs before coating with flour. This produces a plumper, batter-fried oyster.

PICKIN' OYSTER STEW

Wherever the water is the right depth and there's something firm (such as old shells) to attach to, oysters grow in the tidal waters that surround Daufuskie and snake throughout the South Carolina Lowcountry. At low tide, the oysters lie dry on mud flats or attached to rocks or pilings, ripe for picking by anyone willing and able to do some hard work.

During the colder months, when the time was right, Momma and Pop couldn't wait to gather some of the tasty shellfish. They both loved oysters and enjoyed picking and shucking them.

Often, they shared what they gathered, even taking orders to pick and shuck oysters for other islanders who weren't able or willing to gather

Workers move oysters inside for cold storage and shucking at the Bluffton Oyster Company, which is similar to the now-closed factory on Daufuskie that employed many islanders until the 1950s.

their own. And many times they would bundle up my sisters and me against the cold and take us along.

We would make a day of it. As they waded in thick, rubber boots through soft mud to get the oysters at low tide, we built a fire on the shell-covered bluff and played games. We weren't allowed to pick the oysters ourselves, because walking in the soft mud was dangerous. We could easily get stuck, and the oysters were razor sharp. If she had to rescue and doctor us, Momma wouldn't have time to pick and shuck oysters.

As they worked, their hands protected with old socks, they would rinse the mud off the oysters in the water and pass them to us in buckets. We roasted some on the open fire until their shells popped open and we could get at the sweet meat inside. The rest Momma and Pop would shuck on the spot rather than load into a wagon and haul home. They made the hard work look easy as they broke off the "mouth" ends of the oysters and slipped a flattened, sharpened piece of steel, with no handle, between the shells, prying them open and scraping the juicy contents into gallon-size cans. They sat on a wooden bench as they shucked and told us stories of "dem ol' days."

Whether you shuck them yourself or buy them in a tub at the supermarket, oysters are mighty tasty in this stew Momma used to cook on her woodstove.

3 strips bacon
2 tablespoons cooking oil or bacon grease
2 tablespoons flour
2 cups oysters (washed and drained)
1 small onion, diced
1½ cups water
salt and black pepper to taste

Fry the bacon in a skillet. Remove the bacon when it is done, but leave the grease in the pan over medium-high heat. Add the oil and flour, stirring constantly until the flour browns. Add the cooked bacon, oysters, onion, and water. Stir to combine, add salt and pepper to taste, cover, and simmer 10 to 15 minutes. Serve over stiff grits.

The Yard

4

When I was coming up, we lived on several different properties, all owned by Momma's or Pop's families. We lived on the north end of 'Fuskie, and we lived on the south end.

Islanders weren't strict about property lines—except on one old plantation owned by folks from across the water. As children, we wandered where we wanted, and folks didn't worry about vandalism, because they didn't build resentment with fences. We put up fences to keep animals in, not to keep people out. And when someone's cow got loose, a neighbor would let the owner know where it was—or simply return it.

Although Momma always had one or two small flower beds (often with conch shell borders) in the front yard, and almost everyone had a hydrangea bush or two, our yards could never have been confused with English gardens. Cattle tied to trees grazed among the daffodils each spring. Chickens pecked at scratch feed tossed out the back door. Hogs spent much of their time in a pen well away from the house, but each fall we let them out to root in the garden and yard, where they kept grubs and weeds under control while finding potatoes we missed and clearing rotting fruit and nuts from under the trees. When the grass got long in one part of the yard, we just moved one of the cows to a nearby tree. Their grazing kept most snakes away, and we never had to mow the lawn.

We also raised turkeys, guinea hens, ducks, and a few geese, and we always had a couple of dogs and a cat or two. Someone walking in the yard would set off the dogs, and their barking would start the rooster to crowing, the geese to honking, the guineas to whining, and the turkeys to gobbling. If a snake crawled into a nesting box—day or night—the chickens would start the riot. More than a few times, we had to get up in the middle of the night to kill a snake or other varmint and quiet the yard down. I remember Pop cussing and stumbling out the door into the dark with his shotgun. We would chase behind him with a flashlight to see what was going to happen. And I remember Pop sending my sisters and me out alone as we grew older. Huddled together, with hoes and rakes as weapons, we would creep into the chicken coop and squeal louder than the hens cowering in the corner as we chopped at a snake bulging with eggs or chased a coon across the fence.

Except for the dogs and cats, which helped keep the others in line, just about all of the animals sooner or later were headed for Momma's stove. Like the river, the woods, and the garden, the yard was somewhere we looked to for food. We ate eggs from the chickens, drank milk from the cow, and lovingly raised the other animals until their time came. We loved to play with the chicks and ducklings, but only a few ended up as pets. The same went for the other birds and the pigs.

That wasn't so true for our cattle. Killing a cow was a big thing, involving most of our neighbors, who were needed to help do the butchering, share the meat, and open up freezer space. And that was probably why we didn't eat much beef, unless we had just come from a shopping trip to the mainland. Instead, we butchered the smaller animals, which grew more quickly and took up less room in the freezer. Our cows gave us milk or helped with the hard labor and transportation. They became pets. We couldn't even think of eating Bobby, the work "cow" (actually a steer), who pulled our plow and wagon. Eventually, when he was very old, we sold him to a man on nearby Hilton Head Island.

We played in the yard, often with the animals who lived there. And we worked there, too. "Balance" is the word that comes to mind—and "responsibility." Our animals gave us pleasure while causing us work. They mowed our grass and cleaned up fruit under the trees, which saved us work and helped fatten them for our table. We had to feed them twice each day and keep them healthy. And they gave us food when the time came. It was our way of life, and their lives, too. It was different from picking up a package from the cooler in a supermarket, but it fed us well.

As Pop used to say to us on a cold winter morning when we didn't want to slop the hogs or move the cow, "Y'all chillen need to famemba: if ya take care of dem dey animals, dey gonna take care ya."

PORK CHOPS WITH GRAVY

We always had plenty of chores, whatever the season. Feeding and caring for our farm animals topped the list. They relied on us as much as we relied on them for our food.

Slopping the hogs and pigs was not our favorite work. The hog pen was near the woods, a distance from the house. Although it was hard work to carry the heavy buckets of food, we knew how to make it fun when our parents went out.

"Y'all churn make sho ya slop dem hogs," Momma would say as she got ready to go fishing with Pop. "It's almost feedin' time, an' I know y'all can hear dem hollerin'."

The hogs, who would whine for their food at sunup and sundown, were always glad to see us when we came to their pen. With Momma and Pop gone, we'd give the hogs a little food, then hop into the pen and onto the bigger ones' backs while they rooted in the feeding trough.

"Giddyup," we'd cry as they raced around trying to shake us off. After they tossed us in the mud, we would play with the little newborn pigs, squealing with laughter as they squealed at us.

If Momma and Pop caught us—and they did a few times when they heard the hogs bellowing from a distance—they would have our hides. "Good thing the hogs can't talk," we'd say to each other when we got away with our rodeos.

Pork was a great part of our diet, and we cooked with it a lot, whether it was served separately or added to something for flavoring.

I remember hog-killing time, when a neighbor or two would come over to give Pop a hand. We would all watch as they cleaned the hog, dunked it in an old steel drum filled with boiling water to remove the hair from the hide, and hung it from a tree to dry for an hour or two. Next, they would cut it into many chunks, making sure most islanders got at least a small piece.

Anyone who killed something or had a big catch from the river would do the same. Sharing was part of being neighborly. And almost every part of the hog was used for some kind of meal, even down to its hooves, which, mixed with garlic and gin, gave us medicine for colds.

4–6 pork chops
sprinkle salt and black pepper
sprinkle paprika
½ cup flour
⅓ cup cooking oil
1 medium onion, chopped
½ medium bell pepper
1½ cups water

Wash the pork chops and sprinkle them with salt, pepper, and paprika. Put the chops and the flour in a bag, shake, remove the chops, and shake off excess flour. Put the oil in a skillet and place over medium-high heat. To check the oil temperature, drop in a dab of flour, which should brown but not burn. Add the chops to the oil and fry until golden brown on each side (2 to 4 minutes per side). Remove the cooked chops and drain the grease, but don't clean the pan. Add the chopped onion and bell pepper, and stir over heat for about a minute. Add the cooked chops, pour in the water, and cook until the gravy thickens. Serve with rice, potatoes, or noodles. And you might want some bread to soak up every bit of the gravy.

BARBECUE SPARERIBS

15–20 sparerib pieces
sprinkle salt and black pepper
sprinkle paprika
¼ cup cooking oil
1 medium onion, sliced
1 stalk celery, chopped
1 medium green bell pepper, cut into wedges
2 cups hot water
barbecue sauce (make your own or buy some you like)

Buy cut-up spareribs or cut up a slab yourself into pieces that will fit in a medium-large pot. Wash the spareribs and pat dry, then sprinkle them with salt, pepper, and paprika. Put the ribs and oil in the pot. Set the pot over medium heat, add half the onion, celery, and bell pepper, and stir-fry a couple minutes. Add the hot water and boil 20 to 30 min-

A hog waits for feeding time in his Daufuskie Island pen.

utes. This will give you tender and juicy ribs. Take the ribs from the pot and place them in a baking pan. Pour the barbecue sauce of your choice, along with the remaining onion, celery, and bell pepper, over the ribs and bake 30 to 45 minutes in a preheated oven at 350°—or grill them over a low fire, brushing with sauce, 10 to 15 minutes. Then sit down for some sweet, tender, finger-lickin' eatin', and take your time, because they are soooo good.

FRIED RIBS

10–15 sparerib pieces
1 cup cooking oil
sprinkle salt and black pepper
1½ cups flour

Buy cut-up ribs or cut them up yourself. Heat the oil in a deep skillet or fryer. Wash the ribs and pat dry, then season with salt and pepper. Place the flour in a bag (paper or plastic) with the ribs and shake to coat well. Remove the ribs from the bag and shake off excess flour. Test the oil temperature by dropping in a dab of flour and adjust the heat so the flour browns, not burns. Add the ribs and fry, turning, until brown all over (2 to 3 minutes). Serve hot or cold, on the table or in a picnic basket.

ROASTER PAN BAKED HAM

1 fresh ham (8–10 pounds)
1 large onion, chopped
1 large green bell pepper, chopped
2 stalks celery, chopped
2 teaspoons minced garlic (about 2 cloves)
1 teaspoon ground thyme
1 teaspoon salt
1 teaspoon black pepper
sprinkle salt and black pepper

Half fill a large pot with warm water. Add the ham, onion, bell pepper, celery, garlic, thyme, salt, and black pepper. Cover and boil over medium heat 30 minutes. Turn the ham over in the pot and boil another 20 minutes to cook and season evenly. Move the ham from the pot to a roaster pan, pour the broth over the ham, and sprinkle lightly with salt and pepper. Bake in a preheated oven at 350° for about 45 minutes, basting with the gravy every 15 minutes until the ham is browned and tender. Allow to cool before slicing. Serve in a sandwich or with rice or potatoes and gravy from the pan.

DOWN-HOME CHITLINS

Chitlins are an old Southern favorite—especially at Thanksgiving and Christmas. An Englishman might call them chitterlings, but *Webster's* is clear that "chitlins" is proper when you're cooking up hog intestines in our neck of the woods.

Momma and Pop, and most grown-up islanders, loved them. We children weren't too sure. But anyone will tell you, the thing about chitlins is that they have to be cleaned right. If they aren't, the smell of them cooking will run you out of the house. Forget eating them if they smell like that. My Momma really had a way of cleaning chitlins. When neighbors slaughtered a hog, they'd trade half their chitlins just to have her clean them. And we were her helpers.

Momma would place the fresh chitlins (from a local slaughter or from the farmers' market in Savannah) in a big galvanized tub under the mulberry tree or some other tree that needed some fertilizing. Beside the tub she'd dig a shallow hole and line up three clean 5-gallon plastic buckets. She filled two buckets halfway with warm water and left the third to hold the cleaned chitlins.

First, she cut the chitlins into foot-long pieces. Then, for each piece, she held the end and slid the piece between her thumb and finger, squeezing out the contents into the hole beside her. Next, she took a freshly shaved green stick and stuck it a half inch into each chitlin and pulled the chitlin inside out, back over the stick. Momma rinsed the chitlin piece by repeatedly dunking it in the first bucket. Then she peeled the fatty lining from the inside-out chitlin, dropped the lining back into the galvanized tub, dunked the chitlin piece several times in the second bucket, and placed it in the third.

My sisters and I stood by, frowning at the odor and changing the water in the buckets when Momma told us to. When she was done, we covered the hole and emptied the tub and buckets in the woods, where the local animals would have a feast. Momma would wash the chitlins many more times in the kitchen and cut them into 2-inch pieces.

We washed ourselves.

1 gallon cleaned chitlins, cut into 2-inch pieces
3 strips fatback bacon
1 medium onion, chopped
1 medium green bell pepper, chopped
½ teaspoon garlic powder or minced garlic
1 teaspoon salt
½ teaspoon black pepper
2 cups warm water

Clean the chitlins properly and drain thoroughly. Fry the fatback (or any bacon) in a medium pot; when the bacon is done, leave the grease in the pot and turn down the heat. Add the chitlins, onion, bell pepper, garlic, salt, and black pepper. Stir-fry the mixture over medium heat 5 to 10 minutes. Add the water and simmer over medium heat, stirring occasionally, for about an hour, until tender. Most folks eat a bowl full, and many come back for more.

SLOPPIN' TROTTERS (PIGS' FEET)

4–6 fresh pigs' feet, split and cleaned
1 large onion, chopped
1 medium green bell pepper, chopped
1 stalk celery, chopped
1 teaspoon salt
1 teaspoon black pepper

Clean the pigs' feet by scraping with a paring knife under running water. Add to a medium pot two-thirds filled with water and boil 10 to 15 minutes. Drain and rinse with cold water. Return the pigs' feet to the pot, fill the pot halfway with warm water (4 to 6 cups), and add the onion, bell pepper, celery, salt and pepper. Cover and boil for an hour or more, until the pigs' feet are tender. Add warm water as needed to maintain the gravy. Serve alone, over rice, or with bread to soak up every drop of tasty gravy.

PIG TAILS WITH TOMATOES

1½ pounds pig tails, cut into 2-inch pieces
1 small can (6 ounces) tomato paste or
2 14½-ounce cans stewed tomatoes
1 large onion, chopped
salt and black pepper to taste
4 medium potatoes, peeled and halved

Boil the pig tails about 15 minutes in a medium pot, half filled with water. Drain and rinse with warm water. Return the tails to the pot, half filled with fresh, warm water, and add the tomatoes (or tomato paste), onions, and a little salt and pepper. Cover and boil about 45 minutes, stirring occasionally, until the pig tails are tender and the gravy thickens. Adjust the seasoning to taste. Add the potatoes and simmer about 15 minutes, stirring every 5 minutes, until the potatoes are tender but not mushy. Serve alone in a bowl or over rice.

 NECK BONE, TADA, AND TOMATO SOUP

1 pound fresh pork neck bone
½ pound smoked pork neck bone
2 14½-ounce cans stewed tomatoes
1 large onion, chopped
1 stalk celery, chopped
1 medium green bell pepper, chopped
salt and black pepper to taste
4 medium potatoes, peeled and quartered

Place the fresh and smoked neck bones in a large pot, half filled with warm water, and boil 15 minutes. Drain and rinse the neck bones in warm water. Return them to the pot, half filled with fresh warm water, then add the tomatoes, onion, celery, and bell pepper. Cover and boil 45 to 60 minutes, stirring occasionally, until the meat is tender. Add salt and pepper to taste, and toss in the potatoes. Simmer until the potatoes are tender, not mushy, stirring occasionally. Serve in a bowl by itself or over rice.

 LOWCOUNTRY OXTAILS WITH HAM HOCKS

2 ham hocks, split in half
8–10 oxtail pieces
1 large green bell pepper, chopped
1 large onion, chopped
1 stalk celery, chopped
salt and pepper to taste

Put the ham hocks and oxtail pieces in a medium pot, two-thirds full with water, and boil about 15 minutes. Drain and rinse the meat under running water. Return the oxtail and ham hocks to the pot and refill with water as before. Add the bell pepper, onion, and celery. Add salt and pepper to taste. Boil until all the meat is tender (2 hours or more). You may need to add more water to the meat before it is done, but don't add more than 1 to 3 additional cups, because you want the gravy to be rich. Serve with rice or potatoes, and be ready for some lip-lickin' grub.

FIXIN' AND MIXIN' MEATLOAF

Momma kept an old meat grinder hidden on a top shelf in the kitchen. When she had chunks of meat to grind, she would reach up, pull it down, and attach its built-in clamp to the end of the wooden kitchen table.

"Come yah one o' y'all churn," she would yell. As my sisters and I ran into the kitchen to see what she wanted, our faces would light up as we spotted the meat grinder. Momma didn't like to grind the meat, because it worked her elbow and back too hard. But she knew we loved to use the grinder, and we had plenty of energy to burn off. "Wash ya hands before ya touch dis yah," she'd say. "Ah need some meat grind and I don' wan' no playin'."

We were glad for some inside work instead of the hot, heavy chores outside, and we knew a little play mixed with work made it easy. But Momma would warn us our fingers could get caught in the grinder. And she would glance over from her work every chance she had, as the three of us took turns. One of us cranked the handle, another put the meat into the top of the grinder, and the third watched the other two closely, with a critical eye that rivaled Momma's. In no time, we would have all the meat ground. Momma would thank us and send us back to our other chores, with the 'roma of Momma's meatloaf distracting us as dinnertime neared.

1 medium onion, diced
1 medium green bell pepper, diced
1 stalk celery, diced
2 pounds ground beef
½ cup bread crumbs
¼ cup tomato ketchup (+ extra for coating)
2 eggs, beaten
1 teaspoon salt
1 teaspoon black pepper

Combine all of the ingredients in a bowl. Grease a loaf pan and place the mixture in the pan. Coat the top of the loaf with additional ketchup and bake in a preheated oven at 350° for 25 to 30 minutes, depending on how well done you like your meat.

HOMEY BEEF STEW

1½ pounds stew beef
2 tablespoons cooking oil
4 cups warm water
1 can (14½ ounces) whole tomatoes
1 can (6 ounces) tomato paste
1 large onion, chopped
1 large green bell pepper, chopped

1 stalk celery, chopped
1 cup fresh or frozen lima beans
½ cup sweet peas (frozen or canned)
3 fresh ears corn, broken in half
2 medium carrots, cut into 1-inch pieces (or 10 baby carrots)
3 potatoes, peeled and quartered
1 teaspoon sugar
salt and black pepper to taste

Cut the beef into bite-size cubes. Place the beef and the oil in a large stew pot and stir, over medium heat, until brown. Add the water, tomatoes, tomato paste, onion, bell pepper, and celery. Cover and let the mixture boil, stirring occasionally, about 30 minutes. Add the lima beans, peas, and corn, then continue cooking another 15 to 20 minutes, until the meat is tender. Lower the heat and add the carrots, potatoes, sugar, salt, and pepper. Simmer about 30 minutes, until the carrots and potatoes are tender but not mushy. Serve on a plate or in a bowl, with cornbread or biscuits to soak up every drop.

SMUTTERED CUBE STEAK

3–6 medium (8–10 ounce) cube steaks
sprinkle salt and black pepper
1 cup flour
1½ cups cooking oil
1 medium onion, chopped
1 medium green bell pepper, chopped
2 cups warm water

Season the steaks on both sides with salt and pepper. Place the steaks and the flour in a paper or plastic bag and shake to coat the steaks evenly. Remove the steaks and shake off excess flour. Heat the oil in a large skillet; add the steaks and brown on both sides. Remove the steaks from the skillet and drain off all but about 1 tablespoon of oil. Add the onion and bell pepper, and stir-fry for several minutes. Add the steaks and warm water, along with more salt and pepper to taste. Simmer until the gravy thickens. Serve over rice or stiff grits.

 OL'-FASHION POT ROAST

8-pound beef roast (rump, chuck, or round)
¼ cup cooking oil
2 tablespoons flour
1 large onion, chopped
1 medium green bell pepper, chopped
1 stalk celery, chopped
1 teaspoon salt
1 teaspoon black pepper
3 cups water
3 potatoes, peeled and halved
2 carrots, quartered (or 8–10 baby carrots)

In a large pot, brown the meat on all sides in the oil. Remove the meat and drain all but 2 tablespoons of oil and grease from the pot. Add the flour to the pot and cook a few minutes to brown. Return the meat to the pot and add the onion, bell pepper, celery, salt, black pepper, and water. Cover and boil about 45 minutes, turning the meat three times so it will cook evenly. Stick a fork in the meat to check the tenderness. If the

A steer pauses from grazing beside Grandmomma's house.

fork won't go into the meat without force, cook some more. Add the potatoes and carrots, and cook about 20 minutes more, until the potatoes and carrots are tender, not mushy. Serve alone or with rice and additional vegetables.

 COUNTRY-FRIED LIVER WITH ONIONS

4 pieces (4–6 ounces each) liver (beef, calf, pork, or deer)
sprinkle salt and black pepper
½ cup flour
¾ cup cooking oil
1 large onion, sliced in rings

Rinse and pat dry the pieces of liver, then sprinkle them with salt and pepper. Place the flour and liver in a bag (paper or plastic) and shake, coating each piece of liver well. Remove the liver, shaking excess flour from each piece. Heat the oil in a medium skillet and test the temperature with a pinch of flour, which should brown, not burn, when dropped into the hot oil. Add the floured liver to the pan and fry over medium-high heat, turning, until browned on both sides. Remove the cooked liver from the pan and set it on paper towels to drain excess grease. Stir-fry the sliced onions in the same oil about 2 minutes, until the rings are clear. Place the cooked onions on the paper towels with the liver. Allow to drain a minute or so, then serve immediately with grits, rice, or mashed potatoes.

RUNAWAY FRIED CHICKEN

Momma knew every one of her chickens. And she knew when each bird's time was up.

I must have been 11 or 12, the oldest among us girls left at home, when early one morning Momma joined Pop as he set out for the river. Before leaving, she threw some scratch corn out in the yard, and while the chickens were eating, she grabbed a young hen and set her alone in a special coop.

"Sallie Ann," she said, "dis yah chicken is fo' dinnah. Kill it, clean it, and fix it, da way I show ya."

And off they went. I had never killed a chicken before, but I had watched Momma. I knew I was ready for the job. With my wide-eyed little sisters watching, I reached into the coop and grabbed the young hen by the feet. I wrapped my hand around her neck and started swinging that chicken, just as I remembered Momma doing. My problem was that I was swinging the *whole* chicken, and not breaking its neck. Wings were flapping, feathers were flying, and my sisters were screaming, "Let it go!"

So I did.

That chicken hit the ground running, cleared the yard, and was in the woods before we knew what happened. And she wasn't coming back, either.

Since Momma knew her chickens, she would've had my hide if I'd tried to catch another instead. It took us several hours to drive that bird from the thick bushes, hem her in the corner of the fence, and capture her with a scoop net. I grabbed the bird and let my sisters chop her head off with the ax.

When Momma came home, the meal was ready, and she never knew what had happened.

A mother hen and chicks in a Daufuskie yard.

1 young chicken, plucked, cleaned, and cut into parts
sprinkle paprika
sprinkle salt and black pepper
1½ cups cooking oil
1½ cups flour

Season the cleaned chicken with paprika, salt, and pepper. Heat the oil in a deep skillet. Flour the chicken by placing it in a bag (paper or plastic) with the flour and shaking to coat. Remove the chicken pieces from the bag and shake off extra flour. Test the oil temperature by dropping in a dab of flour, which should brown, not burn. Add the chicken to the oil. Cook thoroughly, turning occasionally, until golden brown on all sides.

STEWED CHICKEN FEET

1 pound chicken feet
sprinkle salt and black pepper
¼ cup cooking oil
1 medium onion, chopped
1 stalk celery, chopped
1 medium green bell pepper, chopped
2½ cups warm water

Scrape and peel the scales from the chicken feet, wash thoroughly, and drain. Lightly sprinkle the chicken feet with salt and pepper, while the oil is heating in a medium pot. Add the onions, celery, and bell pepper to the hot oil and stir-fry over medium heat about 2 minutes, until the onions are clear. Add the chicken feet and the water, cover, and boil gently 30 to 45 minutes, until the feet are tender and a medium-thick, yellowish gravy has formed. Add extra salt and pepper to taste. Serve over grits or rice, and don't hesitate to pick up the feet so you can suck every bit of goodness from the bones.

YARD-RAISED, OVEN-BAKED CHICKEN

1 whole chicken, plucked, cleaned, and singed
sprinkle salt and black pepper
sprinkle paprika
1 large onion, chopped
½ cup warm water

After plucking and cleaning, a yard chicken must be singed over a flame (most easily produced by lighting a rolled newspaper or paper bag) to remove fine, hairlike feathers. Wash the chicken well, inside and out, in hot (but not burning hot) tap water and drain thoroughly. Pat dry and sprinkle well, inside and out, with salt, pepper, and paprika. Place the chicken in a roaster pan, adding the onion and water around the bird. Cover and cook in a preheated oven at 350° for an hour or longer (or about 45 minutes for a store-bought fryer), basting every 15 minutes. Remove the cover and brown 15 to 20 minutes, basting every 5 minutes. Serve with rice, potatoes, or stuffing.

DOWN YONDAH CHICKEN STEW

Everybody on 'Fuskie had a yard full of chickens. And while we weren't formal about most things, we kept chickens in fenced pens (to protect them from dogs and varmints). To help us find the eggs, we made laying boxes—which the hens used most of the time—and lined them with pine straw.

From the hen that let us know with a cackle she just laid an egg, to the rooster that woke us up, chickens were part of our lives. We even had pet chickens, including one hen that slept in the house, laid an egg each evening in her rag-lined box under the kitchen table, and died of natural causes at a ripe old age.

But most chickens were "fo' grub," as Pop used to say. If they weren't laying or crowing, we'd for sure be cooking them sooner or later. A young pullet made a quick meal fried up in Momma's pan. But older hens and roosters needed longer heat to be tender.

We children had a good old time chasing down the chicken for Momma. When we caught it, Momma would wring its neck and then dunk the dead bird in boiling water to loosen its feathers for plucking. Once she plucked and cleaned the chicken, she would hold it over the fire to singe the fine feathers from its skin. The cleaned bird, along with its giblets and cleaned feet—nothing was wasted—went in the pot for a long day's warming.

1 chicken, cut into pieces
sprinkle salt and black pepper
4 strips bacon
1 stalk celery, chopped
1 large onion, chopped
1 medium green bell pepper, chopped
2 cups warm water
salt and black pepper to taste
1 hot pepper (optional)

Wash the chicken parts and sprinkle them with salt and pepper. In a medium-to-large pot, fry the bacon; as it begins to get done, add the chicken pieces and fry 5 to 8 minutes, stirring constantly. Add the celery, onion, bell pepper, and water—along with a hot pepper, if you like, and salt and pepper to taste—and cook until tender. An old yard chicken might take all day to get there, but a young fryer should be fit for eating in an hour or less. Serve with rice, potatoes, or Grandmomma's woodstove cornbread.

 TURKEY WINGS WITH GRAVY

4–6 turkey wings, cut into 2 pieces each
¼ cup cooking oil
2 tablespoons flour
1 medium green bell pepper, chopped
1 medium onion, chopped
3 cups warm water
½ teaspoon dried thyme
salt and black pepper to taste

Heat the cooking oil in a medium pot. Thoroughly wash and dry the turkey wings. Fry the wings in the oil, over medium heat, turning, until they begin to brown on both sides. Remove the wings; add the flour to the pot and stir as it browns. When the flour is brown, add the wings, bell pepper, onion, and warm water, and bring to a boil, stirring occasionally. Add the thyme, salt, and pepper shortly after the pot starts to boil. Turkey wings should cook until they're tender, 45 to 60 minutes or more. Add warm water as needed to maintain a rich gravy. Serve with rice or potatoes, or just eat them alone.

BARBECUE TURKEY WINGS

4–6 turkey wings
sprinkle salt and black pepper
1 large onion, sliced into rings
1½ cups barbecue sauce (bottled or homemade, as you prefer)

Wash and drain the turkey wings. Tuck (or fold) the tips into the joints of the wings. Sprinkle the wings lightly with salt and pepper and place them in a baking pan. Bake uncovered in a preheated oven at 350° for close to an hour (or grill for about the same time over a low fire), until browned. Spread the onions over the wings and pour on the barbecue sauce. Cover and bake for another 20 to 30 minutes, until tender. Serve with rice, potatoes, or potato salad, or just eat them alone.

5 The woods

The woods were all around us on Daufuskie. Like most of the eastern United States, the Sea Islands were once covered by natural forests that were cut down in the 1700s and 1800s for lumber, fuel, and fields. But if you leave such a field alone, it won't be a field for long. And the Daufuskie of my childhood had been left alone a long time.

Tall pines, hickories, gums, and oaks, with thick underbrush, grew right up to the edges of our dirt roads. Paths through the woods were marked by deer tracks and formed by our trips to gather firewood. And it was a constant effort to keep our yard and garden from being overgrown by thick woods and underbrush.

As little girls, we learned early that the woods meant danger. There were ticks and chiggers to chew on us, snakes to avoid, big spiders, poison ivy, thorny bushes and briars, and even bobcats. Momma and Pop taught us early to avoid all these things, and we were allowed to play in the woods, so long as we listened to their warnings. We made tree houses, played cowboys and Indians, swung on grape vines (screaming like Tarzan), and gathered Spanish moss to feed to the cows, who loved it. One time, Pop rescued three baby squirrels, who had lost their mother, from a big oak tree on the edge of our yard. We raised them as pets, teaching them to climb trees, and one survived to go back to the wild.

Pop taught us to track deer and rabbits by their droppings and footprints. We learned how to spot "coon roads" by looking for the coons' handlike tracks, trampling of the underbrush, and digging for grubs. And we became Pop's scouts, letting him know where the game was.

Pop also knew we would be curious about his old shotgun and the guns that boys on the island would get on their twelfth or thirteenth Christmas. And Pop also knew he couldn't watch us every minute. So when I was 11 or 12—against Momma's better judgment—Pop set some cans atop the chicken fence post, showed me how to hold his shotgun, and then convinced me to pull the trigger.

The blast nearly knocked me off my feet. My shoulder stung with pain, and I hollered and nearly dropped the gun. But he made me shoot it again, this time holding it more firmly. I hurt for days, but I had respect after that for all firearms. From that day on, Momma and Pop didn't worry as much about leaving us alone. And when we went out hunting with our male cousins, we knew how to be safe.

All island men hunted regularly. The meat they harvested was basic to many of our meals, and they kept the wildlife in balance. Nothing was wasted. If we killed it, we ate it, or we shared it with our neighbors. And what we couldn't eat, we could use in other ways. We made hat racks from antlers and often dried animal hides. Once I even made a scraggly raccoon hat. After we got a freezer, we would put up deer meat beside our packages of shrimp and fish. And Momma would cure rabbit and coon sometimes and cook it in stews that had a rich taste and aroma.

EIGHT-POINT-BUCK STEW

When the pine straw piled up under the trees, the grapevines went yellow, and the nights called out for a sweater or jacket, Pop and his buddies would start cleaning their old guns.

Even clean, the barrel on Pop's old shotgun was rusty, and its stock was beat up. But he could still shoot it at a deer, and every couple years, he'd hit one.

Pop would see deer tracks among his battered corn stalks or spot a trail crossing the dirt road and get all excited. "Dem footprints big as mah hand," he would tell his friends. "We gotta git 'im." Momma would hear the talk about who was "gonna kill" that granddaddy of all deer, and call out, "Y'all be careful," as they headed out the front gate. Pop would fire back: "Ya jest sharpen' up da knife, Bertha, 'cause we gonna eat deer liva fo' suppa."

More times than not, Pop would come back with a few shells of buckshot gone, complaining, "Dat buggah got away. He turn his white tail on me and dug up dirt." But at some point during the fall and winter months, Pop and his buddies would show up at the gate, just after dark, with a deer dangling by its legs from a pole carried between them. Momma would smile as they hoisted the deer up in the old mulberry tree out back, then bled, gutted, and skinned it. Pop would nail the rack of antlers beside others on the tree trunk. More racks like it held hats and coats by our front and back doors. Pop and each of his buddies would get a leg and a share of the tender midsection—but not before opening a jug of moonshine. Whoever brought the deer down would take a swig and brag about what a good shot he was. The others would agree and take a swig themselves.

Sometimes Momma would fry up a piece of meat for everyone. Other times, the men would rush home with their share of the meat for their wives to cook, and Momma would serve supper when they left. Either way, the hunters, with full bellies and foggy heads, would sleep well that night.

2 pounds deer meat
1 teaspoon salt
1 teaspoon black pepper
1 tablespoon minced garlic or garlic powder
1 teaspoon ground thyme
2 tablespoons cooking oil
1 medium onion, chopped
1 medium green bell pepper, chopped
2–3 cups warm water

Wash the deer meat, dry it, dice it into bite-size pieces, and place it in a bowl. Sprinkle the salt, pepper, garlic, and thyme over the meat and mix everything together with your hands. Heat the oil in a medium saucepan. Add the meat to the hot oil and fry, stirring occasionally, until brown. Add the onion, bell pepper, and water, then cook over medium heat until the meat is tender—1 to 2 hours, depending on the deer (larger ones are tougher). Season to taste and add more water as needed to make a thin-to-medium gravy for serving over rice, grits, or potatoes.

DEER ROAST

10–12 pounds deer meat (leg, shoulder, or thigh)
1 teaspoon salt
1 teaspoon black pepper
1 tablespoon minced garlic or garlic powder

1 large onion, chopped
2 stalks celery, chopped
1 medium green bell pepper, chopped
2–3 cups warm water

Wash the meat and place it in a large pot with all the other ingredients. Boil 45 minutes or longer, until the meat is tender enough to stick a fork in easily. Put the entire contents of the pot in a roaster pan. Bake in a preheated oven at 350° for 30 to 45 minutes, basting every 15 minutes. Serve with rice or potatoes. And leftovers make wonderful sandwiches, cold or hot.

SOUTHERN DEER BURGER

2 pounds ground deer meat
½ teaspoon salt
½ teaspoon black pepper
½ tablespoon minced garlic or garlic powder
1 medium onion, diced
1 medium green bell pepper, diced
2 eggs, beaten
¼ cup cooking oil

Combine all of the ingredients except the oil in a bowl, and squeeze with your hands until evenly mixed. Shape into half-pound burgers (roughly a fist-sized ball of meat, flattened). Heat the oil in a medium skillet and fry the burgers, turning, until done (rare, medium, or well, depending on what you like).

OL' FIELD FRIED RABBIT

Like most places in the Carolina Lowcountry, Daufuskie is rotten with wild cottontail rabbits. "Dem critters sho'nuff is a nuisance," Pop used to say as he looked at a row of green stubs that had been corn seedlings a day earlier.

As children, we thought getting rid of that nuisance was real fun. We'd take the yard dogs with us into the woods. They'd lead the way, their noses alert for the scent of a rabbit trail. Sometimes they would come up on a bush or clump of tall grass and start sniffing around. Other times, they'd flush out a rabbit that would dart under a bush. We'd beat the bushes with sticks until a rabbit jumped out. The dogs would be on them quickly, chasing them down and killing them for us. Once in a while the dogs would find a rabbit hole in an old tree. We'd take some dry moss and leaves and make a fire at the mouth of the hole. When the rabbit jumped out, the dogs would do their job—or if Pop was along, he might shoot the critter with his shotgun.

One time, when I was five, I spotted a rabbit in the old field across from our house, where the cattle used to graze. I walked slowly toward him, and he didn't move. When I got close, he took off, hopping in a zigzag across the short grass. I was too young to know I couldn't catch him. And I did. With a flying leap, I dove on him. I was little and he seemed big, scuffling and screaming to get away, but I wasn't giving up. I dug my little hands deep in his soft fur and held on tight, carrying my shivering prize back to the house. We kept him a week until he escaped from the old cage we put him in.

One dog, She-wee, a shepherd mix, caught rabbits on her own. She earned her name as the runt of her litter, but she grew up big and loved all us chillen. Several mornings each week, she would greet us on the front porch, all proud, standing over a fresh-killed rabbit. By dinnertime, that rabbit would be poppin' in grease.

As Pop used to say, "Dem critters been eatin' on my garden. Now I'm gonna be eatin' on dem."

1–2 medium rabbits (skinned, gutted, and cut up)
sprinkle salt and black pepper
1½ cups bacon grease and/or cooking oil
1½ cups flour

After the fun of catching and cleaning the rabbit, cut it into parts, much as you would a chicken. Wash well and pat dry with a cloth, then season with salt and pepper (and other seasonings—I sometimes use garlic or thyme—if you like). Pour the grease and/or oil in a skillet and let it get good and hot (test the temperature by dropping in a dab of flour, which should brown but not burn). Flour the rabbit pieces by placing them in a bag with the flour and shaking to coat, then remove the pieces and shake off excess flour. Place the rabbit in the skillet and fry 2 to 4 minutes, turning often, until golden brown and tender.

SMUTTERED RABBIT

1 rabbit, cleaned and cut up
sprinkle salt and black pepper
¾ cup cooking oil
½ cup flour
1 medium onion, chopped
1 medium green bell pepper, chopped
2 cups warm water

A dirt road snakes through the Daufuskie woods.

Wash the rabbit pieces, pat dry, and sprinkle lightly with salt and pepper. While the oil heats in a medium skillet, put the rabbit pieces in a bag (paper or plastic) with the flour and shake to coat; remove the pieces from the bag and shake off excess flour. Test the oil temperature with a dab of flour, which should brown rather than burn when dropped into the hot oil. Add the rabbit to the skillet and fry 2 to 4 minutes, turning often, until medium brown on both sides. Remove the rabbit from the grease and drain the skillet but don't wipe it clean. Stir-fry the onion and bell pepper in the skillet 1 or 2 minutes. Add the fried rabbit pieces and water. Bring to a boil, then lower the heat and simmer until the gravy thickens and the meat is tender, 15 to 25 minutes. Serve over rice, grits, or potatoes, with hand-tossed fluffy biscuits or Grandmomma's woodstove cornbread to sop up every drop of gravy.

FRIED SQUIRREL

There is nothing special about our squirrels on Daufuskie. They're the same crafty little gray squirrels that gardeners cuss at and city folks feed in the parks elsewhere. Like squirrels most everywhere, they're quick learners and know how to get away fast from trouble. On Daufuskie, with hungry folks, their dogs, and even a bobcat or two, trouble was usually nearby.

Also as in most places, young hunters on Daufuskie learned how to hunt by shooting squirrels, and everyone on the island liked eating them. My cousin Carvin, who was two or three years older than me, got his first .410 shotgun when he was about 13. We came up playing in the woods and fields together, and Carvin used what he knew to learn even more about squirrels. He also set up targets, and even let us girls shoot at them with him. Carvin got good.

During the fall and winter, when the squirrels were fat, Carvin would come by our house with a bundle of squirrels strung together with a palmetto leaf and slung over his back. Momma was always happy to see him and his friends. She would pay the going rate among islanders: 50 cents to a dollar for each squirrel, depending on its size.

Carvin is no longer with us. But I still remember his parties. He would tell folks in the morning, "Be at my house tonight. We goin' to do a little cookin'." They would ask what to bring. Carvin would say, "Just be there. By the time I come out the woods, we'll have plenty."

HOW TO CLEAN A SQUIRREL (OR OTHER SMALL MAMMAL)

You can singe (my family used to say "squinge") the hair off a squirrel or you can skin it. Either way is good for stew, and singeing (leaving the skin on) gives a much stronger flavor, but you must skin a frying squirrel. To singe a squirrel, place it over an open fire outdoors and scrape the hair off as it burns. After removing the hair, use a soft brush to clean the skin under running water.

Skinning a squirrel is easy: just insert a sharp knife under a leg, put your finger between the meat and the skin, work it under the skin in all directions, then pull on the skin and it slips right off. Next, you cut open the squirrel from the neck on down, remove all unwanted parts inside, clean the carcass well, and cut into 2 or 4 parts for cooking.

3–4 squirrels, skinned, cleaned, and cut up
sprinkle salt and black pepper
½ cup flour
¾ cup cooking oil

Wash the squirrel pieces, pat dry, and sprinkle lightly with salt and pepper. Place them in a bag (paper or plastic) with the flour and shake until the pieces are coated evenly; remove and shake off excess flour. Meanwhile, heat the oil in a medium skillet and test the temperature with a dab of flour (it should brown but not burn when dropped into the oil). Fry the squirrel pieces 2 to 4 minutes in the hot oil, turning, until golden brown. Allow pieces to drain on a paper towel. Serve hot with bread and/or rice.

NATIVE SQUIRREL STEW

4–6 cleaned squirrels, cut into pieces
1 piece fatback bacon
sprinkle salt
sprinkle black pepper
1 medium onion, chopped
1 medium green bell pepper, chopped
1 stalk celery, chopped
1½ cups hot water

Fry the fatback in a medium pot; when it's done, remove and set aside, leaving the grease in the pot. Season the squirrel pieces with salt and pepper, then place them in the pot with the hot bacon drippings, being careful of the popping grease. Add the chopped onion, bell pepper, celery, fried fatback, and water. Add salt and pepper to taste, then cook on medium heat 30 to 60 minutes, until the squirrel is tender.

BACKWOODS BAKED BARBECUE COON

Bandit-faced raccoons are found only in North America. But there's no shortage of them—both in wilder places like Daufuskie and in most cities, where "gourmet coons" raid only certain restaurants' trash cans. They're smart and playful but, when they want or need to be, are fierce fighters. A full-grown coon can top 20 pounds and, if cornered, take on most dogs.

As children, we raised several small coons as pets. We learned they have paws like hands to help them get into anything—or out of most things, including their cages. They also will eat most anything—animal or vegetable.

But if there was one kind of eatin' almost all folks on 'Fuskie loved, it was coon. When Pop would stumble on a "coon trail" of handlike tracks, he'd come home all charged up. "Bertha," he'd holler to Mama, "gimme 'dat coon trap." He or Mama would take a leg-hold trap, and with fish as bait, set it at dusk along the coon's path. If the crafty, night hunter hadn't stolen our bait, Pop would find dinner waiting in the trap at dawn.

1 medium-to-large raccoon
sprinkle salt and black pepper
¼ cup cooking oil
1 medium onion, chopped
1 medium green bell pepper, chopped
1 stalk celery, chopped (optional)
4–5 cups water
1 cup barbecue sauce (of your choice)

After skinning, gutting, and cleaning, cut the coon into portions (leg, thigh, ribs, etc.), sprinkle with salt and pepper, and, in a large pot, partially fry (3 to 4 minutes) in oil. Drain the excess oil and fat. Add the onion, bell pepper, celery, and water to the pot. Parboil about 45 minutes to help tenderize. Remove the meat and vegetables from the pot and place in a baking pan. Coat each piece of meat with barbecue sauce and bake 20 to 30 minutes in a preheated 350° oven. Serve with rice or alone in all its greasy glory. As home folks used to say, "Dem coon dey be mighty good eatin'."

POT FULL O' COON

1 raccoon, skinned, cleaned, and cut into pieces
sprinkle salt and black pepper
sprinkle garlic powder
3 pieces fatback bacon
1 medium onion, chopped
1 medium green bell pepper, chopped
3 cups warm water

Remove any excess fat from the coon pieces, then wash, pat dry, and sprinkle lightly with salt, pepper, and garlic powder, while the fatback fries in a large pot. Add the coon pieces to the hot grease and stir-fry 5 minutes or longer, until browned. Add the onion, bell pepper, and water. Cover and boil 30 to 45 minutes, stirring regularly, until the meat is tender. Serve in a bowl, over rice or grits, with collard greens on the side.

BAKED POSSUM

1 possum
3 strips bacon
1 stalk celery, chopped
2 medium onions, chopped (divided)
1 medium green bell pepper, chopped
sprinkle salt and black pepper
sprinkle minced garlic or garlic powder
3–4 cups warm water

After you singe and gut the possum, scrape off the remaining hair, scrub the possum with a stiff brush, and rinse it thoroughly. Cut off any excess fat and cut the possum into pieces while the bacon fries in a large pot. Add the celery, one of the onions, and the bell pepper to the pot. Fry until lightly browned. Sprinkle the possum with salt, pepper, and garlic powder. Add the possum and water to the pot and boil for about an hour. Remove the possum to a roaster pan and pour the rest of the pot's contents over it. Add the second onion over the possum and season to taste with additional salt, pepper, and garlic. Cover the roaster pan and bake in a preheated oven at 350° for 45 to 60 minutes. Remove the cover and bake another 20 minutes. Serve with rice or potatoes.

Rice Dishes

The South Carolina Lowcountry was built on rice, perhaps even more than on the long-staple Sea Island cotton it was famous for. Rice culture came to the Lowcountry from Africa and the Caribbean, along with the slaves imported to clear the land and tend the cotton and indigo that grew on early plantations. Early on, the plantation owners learned—probably from their slaves—that rice could grow very well in tidal South Carolina.

Some rice was grown even on Daufuskie, although the island is small, with only a few freshwater swamps and ponds where the rice could thrive.

By 1850, the wealthiest men in the world owned plantations between Charleston and Savannah (with other homes in New York, Newport, and even Cape Cod), many just a few miles inland from Daufuskie. Rice fed everyone and made the rich richer. Slaves and mules dug ditches, built berms, and channeled the water from rivers named Savannah, Coosawhatchie, Combahee, Edisto, Ashley, and Cooper, then harvested the grain that the water helped grow. On the backs of this forced labor, the plantation owners built their fortunes.

This rice culture largely ended with the Civil War, but many rice ponds and drainage ditches remain, sketching a pattern across the marshy Lowcountry, just upstream from the salty tides. You can see them from an airplane and cross them on a few highways. One or two gentleman farmers still try to raise some of the golden rice that was famous around the world. But for most of us, rice culture lives on in our pots, not our fields. Rice is basic to many, if not most, of our meals—the way potatoes are in the Midwest.

Once a month we'd go shopping on nearby Hilton Head Island or the mainland, and every two or three months we would bring home a 50-pound cotton sack filled with long-grain white rice.

From that big sack, we filled a large covered can that sat under the kitchen table. Nearly every meal began with a scoop from that can. Two cups of rice, three cups of water, a pinch of salt, and a slow simmer in a covered pot was the rhythm of Momma's kitchen. She would sometimes eat "cakes" of leftover rice (scraped from the bottom of the pot) with clabber (curdled) milk for breakfast. We would whip up "anything rice" with an egg or two for breakfast, lunch, or dinner.

At most meals, rice was a side dish or something to pour gravy or stew over. But we had special meals, and some quick ones, where rice was cooked with other ingredients as long pots or in casseroles—like the group of recipes that follows.

Note that, once you have combined all the ingredients, these rice recipes can be cooked on top of your stove or in the oven (the amount of time required to finish cooking the dish is the same either way). Many folks find it easier to oven-cook rice dishes in a covered casserole or roaster pan, since rice often sticks to a pot on top of the stove.

Pouring rice into a pot over a can like the one Sallie's family used for storing their staple grain.

OL' 'FUSKIE FRIED CRAB RICE

Long as I can remember, crab rice was a monthly treat around our house. As I've raised my own family—sometimes near the water, sometimes not so near—I've cherished this dish and added a few touches of my own. If there's a picnic or a family gathering, I'll find a way to get some crabs. When I find folks with a dock, it's not long before I'll be asking them if I can I set out a crab trap or two. Because as soon as someone tastes ol' 'Fuskie crab rice, they're likely to be asking me to make it.

My kids beg for crab rice all the time, and just as my mother did with us girls, I make them help me pick the crabs. We sit out on the porch or around the kitchen table, spread some newspapers and go to pickin'. The more hands we've got, the sooner we're ready to cook.

1½ cups uncooked rice
2¼ cups warm water
pinch salt
2 strips bacon
¼ cup vegetable oil
1 stalk celery, chopped
1 medium green bell pepper, chopped
1 medium onion, chopped
1½–2 pounds crabmeat (lump and claw)
1 tablespoon garlic powder
salt and black pepper to taste

Measure the dry rice, then rinse and drain it several times. Put it, the warm water, and a pinch of salt in a medium pot. Cover, bring to a boil, and simmer 20 minutes or more, until the rice is done and the water is absorbed. Fry the bacon until crispy in a 12-inch skillet; when the

Willis Simmons cooks crabs—much as Pop used to in Sallie's yard—at a community gathering on Daufuskie.

bacon is done, remove it from the pan, set aside, and crumble when cool. Add the oil to the bacon fat in the skillet, heat, then add the celery, bell pepper, and onion. Stir-fry until the onions are clear, then add the crab and cook another 5 to 10 minutes until the crab begins to brown. Add the crumbled bacon, cooked rice, and garlic powder, along with salt and pepper to taste, and stir constantly until evenly combined. Cover the mixture and simmer for at least 10 minutes. (If you'd like a meatier mixture, just use more crab and less rice.)

OVA DEH SHRIMP AND RICE

Shrimp and rice were each basic to eating on Daufuskie, and this recipe combines them in one pot.

We scooped the rice we needed from a covered can under the kitchen table. And we caught our shrimp as we needed them in homemade cast nets.

Since we weren't, for most of my childhood, boat owners, we had to cast from the shore or from an old dock. On the lower side of rising and dropping tides, we would go down to Cooper River Landing or to one of several creeks that crawl into the ends of Daufuskie.

Pop was the expert. But he would let us cast, too, as soon as we could lift his smallest net and the lead "bullets" that ringed it. That net was 5 feet long—and twice that size when spread open. He knitted nets up to 10 feet long, but they were for other, taller folks with more energy than I had.

In the summer, we caught the biggest shrimp in the narrow channels as the tide emptied the creeks or on the edges of the marsh just as the rising tide touched the grass. As the weather cooled, Pop would sometimes catch them in his deep "mullet holes."

A family casts for shrimp in the May River, a few miles from Daufuskie.

Most times, preparing the meal was a family affair. While the cookstove warmed inside, my older sister and I would sit on the porch and talk as we headed, peeled, and deveined the shrimp.

When we finished, Momma would take the shrimp toward the kitchen, hollering over her shoulder, "Ya two comeyah and wash ya hands." In the hot kitchen, she'd put us to work, showing us every step in the fixin' and mixin'. Her patience was short as she assigned jobs: "Ah'm only gonna show ya once," she'd say, "fo' ya need to know dis."

3 strips fatback bacon
1 medium onion, chopped
½ medium green bell pepper, chopped
1 tablespoon cooking oil
2 tablespoons flour
3 cups warm water
2 cups medium shrimp, peeled and deveined
salt and black pepper to taste
2 cups uncooked rice

Fry the fatback and remove it from the pot when done, leaving the grease. Add the onion and bell pepper, then stir-fry until the onion is clear. Remove the vegetables from the pot and set them aside. Add the oil to the pot; then add the flour and brown over medium heat. Add the fried fatback, water, cooked bell pepper and onion, and shrimp. Cook, stirring often, for about 15 minutes, until the shrimp is pink and a thin sauce forms. Season with salt and pepper to taste. Wash and drain the rice several times, add it to the pot, stir to combine the mixture, and cover. Lower the heat and simmer, stirring occasionally, until the rice is cooked (30 to 45 minutes). Note that this is a very different recipe from those that add cooked shrimp to cooked rice. In this recipe, everything cooks together, mixing flavors for some plumb good eatin'.

OYSTERS AND RICE

4 strips bacon
1 tablespoon cooking oil
1 large onion, chopped
1 medium green bell pepper, chopped
2 tablespoons flour
3 cups warm water
salt and black pepper to taste
2 cups uncooked rice
1 quart shucked oysters, drained

Fry the bacon until crisp in a medium pot. Remove the bacon, leaving the grease in the pot. Add the oil, onion, and bell pepper, and stir-fry until the onion is clear. Remove the onion and bell pepper, leaving the oil and grease. Brown the flour in the oil and grease, then return the bacon, onion, and bell pepper to the pot. Add the water, season to taste with salt and pepper, bring to a boil, lower the heat, and simmer 15 minutes, stirring often, to form a thin gravy. Rinse and drain the rice several times and rinse the oysters, then add both to the pot. Combine thoroughly, cover, and simmer, stirring occasionally, 30 to 45 minutes. Serve as a meal, with vegetable side dishes.

CRACKIN' CONCH AND RICE

3 strips smoked bacon
2 pieces smoked pork neck bone
7 cups warm water (divided)
1 medium onion, chopped
1 medium green bell pepper, chopped
1 pound conch, diced
2 tablespoons cooking oil
2 tablespoons flour
salt and black pepper to taste
2 cups uncooked rice

Fry the bacon in a skillet, then remove, leaving the grease in the skillet. In a different, medium pot, place 3 cups water and the neck bone pieces, boil 15 minutes, and drain. Add the bacon, onion, bell pepper, conch, and 3 cups of water to the pot, note the water level, and bring the mixture to a boil. While the pot warms to a boil, add the oil and flour to the grease in the skillet used earlier to fry the bacon, and stir over medium-high heat until the flour browns. Add the grease and browned flour to the neck bone and conch in the pot. Combine thoroughly, then boil 30 to 45 minutes more, until a thin sauce forms and the conch is tender. Season to taste with salt and pepper, add another cup of warm water, and bring to a boil again. Rinse and drain the rice several times, add it to the pot, and stir well. Cover and simmer 30 to 45 minutes, stirring occasionally, until the rice is fully cooked.

SEAFOOD RICE

3 strips smoked bacon
1 medium onion, chopped
1 medium green bell pepper, chopped
2 14½-ounce cans diced or stewed tomatoes
1 tablespoon tomato paste
3 cups warm water
½ teaspoon dried thyme
½ teaspoon minced garlic or garlic powder
1 pint shucked oysters
½ pound crabmeat (lump and claw)
½ pound shrimp, peeled and deveined
salt and black pepper to taste
2 cups uncooked rice

Fry the bacon in a large pot. When the bacon is about done, add the onion and bell pepper to the grease and stir-fry until the onion is clear. Add the tomatoes, tomato paste, water, thyme, and garlic, then simmer, stirring often, 20 to 30 minutes. Add the oysters, crab, and shrimp, then simmer another 15 minutes. Season to taste with salt and pepper. Wash and drain the rice several times, add it to the pot, stir well, cover, and simmer 30 to 45 minutes, until the rice is done. Add a vegetable side dish, and you have a tasty meal.

GENERATIONS HOPPIN' JOHN

I remember as a little girl trying to stay up to bring in the New Year. Most years, all evening long, we girls—with the aprons Momma made us tied tightly around our waists—worked with Momma in the kitchen to put together a big meal for midnight. Pop and a couple of his buddies would start talking and drinking homemade wine on the porch about sunset. As the evening cooled, they migrated toward the table, where the wood heater warmed the room. Tales of people passed, and the good ol' days grew louder as the hour grew later. About 11 o'clock, Pop's friends would leave, to make sure they were home before the year turned. If they were out anywhere besides church (where many of our neighbors spent New Year's), so the saying went, "dey spend mo' time out dey house den in it" during the coming year.

But even with all the activity around me, I was just too little to hold my eyes open, and I would doze as midnight neared. The sound of Pop's shotgun joining all the neighbors' blasts at midnight would wake my sisters and me. We would gather around the table for a prayer and sit down to the feast we'd been cooking all evening.

On top of Momma's special starched, white holiday tablecloth sat a big bowl of collards, a bowl of chitlins, a baked coon, potato salad, cornbread, sweet tada pie, and the most important dish of all, Momma's famous hoppin' John.

Hoppin' John is an old Southern dish, made with foods that were staples for the earliest settlers and their servants. People from different places make it differently. But most everywhere the dish is associated with New Year's. For generations, our folks believed good luck came from making our first forkful of the year hoppin' John.

On Daufuskie, we made ours with red field peas and lots of meat, all pork. Other folks use black-eyed peas of various varieties and less meat.

But any way or any time you mix it up, hoppin' John is "good fo' da belly and da soul."

1 cup dried field peas (red peas, cowpeas, or black-eyed peas)
2–3 pieces fresh or smoked pork neck bone
2–3 pieces fresh pig tail
2–3 pieces ham hock
½ pound hog jowl, chopped (optional)
4 cups warm water
1 large onion, chopped
salt and black pepper to taste
2 cups uncooked white rice

Put the red peas in a bowl and pick out any bad ones. Add water to the bowl, and other bad peas will float to the top. Remove those bad ones, drain the rest, and rinse two more times. Cover the peas with water again and let them soak in the bowl as you boil the meat. Put the meat in a large stew pot and boil 20 to 30 minutes. Drain, add the water, cover, and boil the meat for another 30 to 45 minutes. Drain the water from the peas in the bowl, add them and the onion to the pot, cover, and boil 1 hour or more, until they are tender. At this point, you should have a very meaty pea soup. Season with salt and pepper to taste. Wash and drain the rice several times, add to the pot, stir well, cover, and simmer 30 to 45 minutes, stirring again two or three times to combine the ingredients, until the rice is fully cooked. Don't stir too much or the rice will get mushy. Then set yourself down, and eat plenty, fo' ya gonna have good luck.

SIZZLIN' SAUSAGE RED RICE

3 strips smoked bacon
2 smoked sausage links
1 large onion, chopped
1 medium green bell pepper, chopped
1 stalk celery, chopped
6-ounce can tomato paste
1 teaspoon sugar
3 cups warm water
salt and black pepper to taste
2 cups white rice, uncooked

You must pay careful attention when cooking red rice, since it can stick to your pot easily and make a big mess instead of some good eating. For that reason, I usually finish mine in the oven. Regardless, first fry the bacon and sausage in a medium pot, and, when they're done, cut them into pieces and set aside. Add the onion, bell pepper, and celery to the grease in the pot and stir-fry 3 to 5 minutes until the onion is clear. Add the tomato paste, sugar, water, and bacon and sausage pieces. Season with salt and pepper to taste. Boil, uncovered, until a medium-thick sauce forms. Wash and drain the rice several times and add it to the pot. Combine thoroughly. Simmer over medium-low heat or put into a covered casserole or baking pan and bake in a preheated oven at 350°. Whether it's on top of the stove or in the oven, stir the mixture every 10 minutes and cook until the rice is tender, usually 30 to 45 minutes.

CHICKEN AND RICE

1 chicken, cut into pieces
3 strips smoked bacon
1 large onion, chopped
2 stalks celery, chopped
1 large green bell pepper, chopped
1 teaspoon salt
1 teaspoon black pepper
1 teaspoon garlic powder
½ teaspoon dried thyme
3½ cups warm water
2 cups uncooked rice

Thoroughly wash the chicken pieces. Fry the bacon in a large pot. As the bacon is getting done, add the onion, celery, and bell pepper, and stir-fry until the onion is clear. Add the chicken pieces, salt, pepper, garlic powder, and thyme, and cook over medium heat 5 minutes, stirring often. Add the water and boil gently for 25 minutes, stirring occasionally. Adjust the seasoning to taste. Rinse and drain the rice several times, then add it to the pot, lower the heat, cover, and simmer for 20 to 30 minutes, until the rice is done. Serve as a meal with a vegetable side dish.

1529
SL-2520-AR

7 Quick Meals

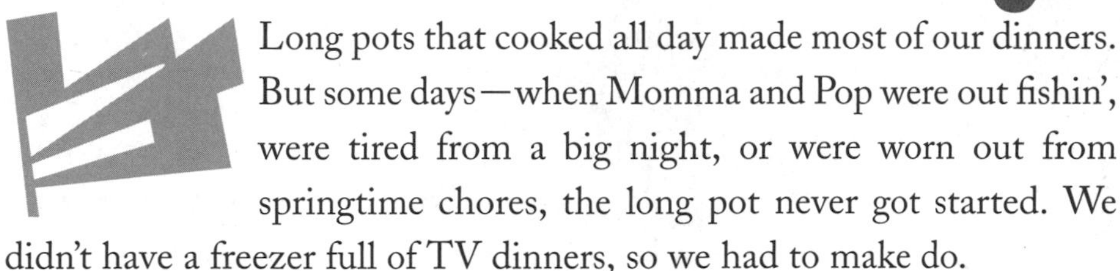

Long pots that cooked all day made most of our dinners. But some days—when Momma and Pop were out fishin', were tired from a big night, or were worn out from springtime chores, the long pot never got started. We didn't have a freezer full of TV dinners, so we had to make do.

Often, we dressed up leftovers from a day or two before. Add a box of elbow macaroni, a can of something from the shelf, or a scoop of rice and we'd be well on our way to fillin' our bellies. Momma had a few standby recipes for such times. But most quick meals were challenges—sometimes adventures—for my sisters and me, who were cooking because our parents weren't home. We would often make up the ingredients as we cooked.

The challenge would begin with the lighting of our woodstove. Momma kept a Clo-White bleach jug filled with kerosene tucked into a corner behind the stove, far enough away so it wouldn't overheat. Now, when Momma was home, she would send us out to find some small branches, wood chips, or pine cones to start the fire logs burning. But when the folks weren't watching, we often took a short cut. Momma's fires only needed a little pour of kerosene. But we knew a few extra pours would save us a trip to the yard or woods. I remember more than a few times touching a match to a soaked stack of wood and tumbling back as flames shot—in a loud "poof"—from openings we didn't even know the stove had. There were singed bangs and eyebrows to explain when Momma came home. And sometimes we'd stand up after the blast, wondering whether we had destroyed the stove. It seemed as if the stove had jumped off the kitchen floor and sat back down. I guess we figured quick meals needed quick fires.

These days, most folks have electric ranges or self-starting gas burners. But parents are busier than ever. Dad often needs to stir up something after a long day of work, or the kids need to cook because Mom's working late. These seven recipes aim to help you through the busy times, just as they did our family.

They offer tasty, belly-fillin', healthy meals that can be prepared in 20 minutes or less, for a few dollars or less. Some recipes include rice or noodles that cook with the other ingredients. For others, you can warm up some leftover rice, grits, or potatoes, or have them cooking while you prepare the rest of the meal.

As Pop used to say, "Disyah grub will stick to ya ribs 'til the next meal comes 'roun'."

ANYTHING RICE

There were times when my sisters and I had to feed ourselves. Momma and Pop would go off to work, hunt, fish, or whatever, and we had to prepare a meal to get us through the hours they were gone.

"Y'all gotta fend fo' ya'self 'til we gets back," Momma would say as she headed out the door. But most times we didn't see this as a chore. We'd have some fun "stirrin' up sumpem dat was belly fillin' fo' da meantime."

Momma and Pop had taught us well how to cook and always made sure there was some food around that we knew how to fix. Some kind of meat was usually left from the previous day, and we almost always had some cooked rice in the icebox. Sometimes Momma would suggest a long pot, but we didn't like that. We wanted to "whup up sumpem we could set down and eat up rightcha." One of my favorite meals was made by finding some leftover meat or fish and some cooked rice, and tossing them in a skillet with whatever caught our fancy. When you're good and hungry, a mixed-up quick meal tastes every bit as good as any long pot. And you don't have to wait.

But it was also a must that we clean up behind ourselves when we finished, or we would not be allowed in the kitchen next time Momma and Pop were gone.

1 tablespoon cooking oil
½ medium green bell pepper, chopped
½ medium onion, chopped
2 eggs, beaten
2 cups cooked rice
leftover chicken, pork chops, hamburger, fish, shrimp, bacon, or whatever

Heat the oil in a skillet. Add the onion and bell pepper and stir-fry 3 minutes. Add the eggs and scramble. Put in the rice and your favorite meat, stir-fry, and the aroma will get your taste buds hungry. Serve immediately for breakfast, dinner, or supper.

A batch of anything rice is moved quickly to the table.

MACARONI AND CHEESE

You can eat only so much rice and so much grits. So once in a while, Momma would stir up some macaroni and cheese for us. Some Sundays, she would even serve it beside the rice with our big dinner.

"Y'all churn go catch da fire in da stove, so dat oven can git hot," she would say. And within the hour her Sunday baking would be in the oven.

For her, macaroni and cheese was often an afterthought. In my house, macaroni and cheese has been a staple side dish. Put it on a plate beside sliced ham or hamburgers, add a salad or some greens, and you have a good meal for a busy weekday evening. Cold in the refrigerator, it's a good snack. Beside a plate of cold fried chicken, it's a picnic.

This recipe is the real thing. And it's not much more trouble than boiling boxed noodles and stirring in some cheesy sauce.

2 cups elbow macaroni
1–1½ pounds cheddar cheese, grated or cut into small pieces
1½ cups milk
1 stick butter or margarine, melted
3–4 large eggs, beaten
½ teaspoon black pepper

Half fill a medium pot with cold water and bring it to a boil. Pour in the macaroni and cook about 10 minutes, so it is firm, not mushy. While the macaroni is cooking, prepare the cheese, butter, and eggs as indicated above. Rinse the cooked macaroni in hot water, then drain. Holding ¼ cup of the cheese in reserve, combine all the ingredients, stir to combine, and pour into a deep baking dish. Stir the ingredients again, then sprinkle the reserved cheese on top. Bake 20 to 30 minutes (bake longer for deeper dishes) in a preheated 350° oven.

PORK AND BEANS WITH SAUSAGE OR BACON

3 links smoked sausage or 4–5 strips bacon
1 medium onion, chopped
2 16-ounce cans pork and beans
1½ cups water
salt and black pepper to taste

Fry the sausage or bacon in a medium skillet. When done, remove, set aside, and stir-fry the onion in the grease until clear. Drain the grease, slice the sausage into pieces, and place all of the ingredients in the skillet. Cover and simmer 15 to 20 minutes. Serve over rice or stiff grits.

SWEET PEAS AND HAMBURGER

2 strips smoked bacon
1 tablespoon cooking oil
1 pound hamburger (lean ground beef)
½ teaspoon salt
½ teaspoon black pepper
1 medium onion, chopped
15-ounce can sweet peas

Fry the bacon in a skillet; when it's done, remove it and set aside, leaving the bacon grease in the skillet. Add the cooking oil to the grease. Mix the hamburger meat with the salt and pepper in a bowl. Add the seasoned hamburger to the oil and grease in the skillet and break it up by stirring as it browns. When the hamburger is almost done, drain the grease and oil, and add the onion and bacon to the skillet. Stir the peas, including the liquid from the can, into the skillet mixture and simmer over medium heat, stirring occasionally, 15 minutes. Serve immediately or hold over low heat.

STEWED TOMATOES WITH HAM

4–6 thick slices of smoked ham
¼ cup cooking oil
2 14½-ounce cans stewed tomatoes
1 medium onion, chopped
1 cup water
salt and black pepper to taste

Add the ham to the oil in a medium skillet and brown on both sides. Drain the oil, add the tomatoes, onion, and water, and season to taste with salt and pepper. Cover and simmer 15 to 20 minutes. Serve over rice, stiff grits, or most any kind of potatoes.

SARDINES WITH BACON

4–5 strips smoked bacon
1 medium onion, chopped
2 14¾-ounce cans large sardines

Fry the bacon in a skillet and drain the grease. Add the onion and the entire contents of the sardine cans to the skillet. Cover and simmer 10 to 20 minutes and serve over stiff grits or rice.

CANNED SALMON WITH BACON AND ONIONS

3–4 strips fatback bacon
1 14¾-ounce can pink salmon
1 medium onion, chopped
½ cup water
salt and black pepper to taste

Fry the fatback until brown in a medium skillet and leave the grease. Add the salmon (don't drain the juice from thc can, but, if you wish, remove some of the skin and bones), onion, and water, and season to taste with salt and pepper. Stir gently, but thoroughly, cover, and simmer 10 to 15 minutes. Serve over rice or stiff grits.

8 Breads & Sweets

Baked goods were always a treat when we were coming up on 'Fuskie. We had store-bought bread only on the days following our monthly trips to Hilton Head Island or Savannah. Most came from the Sunbeam day-old bread store in Savannah, where we paid a dollar to fill a big brown paper bag with white bread, rolls, and snack cakes.

The rest we baked ourselves in Momma's woodstove. And most baking took place on Sundays. Momma would make two pans of cornbread to last into the week. Almost every Sunday, she would also bake a pie, cobbler, or sweet bread. The variety rotated with the seasons.

In the winter, sweet potatoes that had been harvested from the garden in late fall flavored our pies, breads, and pones. By late spring, we could pull carrots from the garden for carrot cake. In late May, Momma would send us into the woods to gather wild blueberries for biscuits. Within a month, we'd be tearing up our ankles among the tough, low vines in the blackberry patches that grew in open, untended parts of the island. By late summer, we'd be picking peaches, pears, and apples from our trees for cobbler, sweet bread, and pie. By early fall, the pumpkins would ripen on long vines in our garden, and they would keep fresh well into the winter, flavoring pies and breads. The walnuts and pecans began falling from our trees about the same time, and all winter long we gathered them. In my memory, the pecans were our only cash crop. Besides cracking them on the porch for a snack or for flavoring a sweet treat, Momma and Pop would sell them at the market when we went across the water and trade them with other folks on the island.

Cornbread or biscuits were a part of most suppers. Momma baked them well, but Pop always liked to think he was the better biscuit maker. You could tell he enjoyed soaking up gravy with her biscuits, but he'd always brag that he would bake them better the next day.

We bought a 25-pound cotton sack of self-rising flour each month when we crossed the water, and it sat in a galvanized trash can, the lid tightly closed, in the corner of Momma's kitchen—right beside the cans of rice and grits. We also purchased sugar, molasses, spices, and canned goods that we would add to our breads and desserts. Nothing went to waste. Stale bread helped make bread pudding. Extra pumpkins and sweet potatoes, along with table scraps, helped fatten our hogs—who in turn helped put the crackle in Momma's cracklin' bread.

Although most desserts were baked, we even had ice cream once in a while. Momma mixed it up from a store-bought ice cream starter pack or with a box of store-bought ice cream as a base. She always added to the mix with fresh milk and cream, sometimes fruit, and anything else we had in the house—until you couldn't even tell there was a packaged product involved. We churned the concoctions by hand, collecting ice from our shopping trips, aging refrigerator, and neighbors.

Like most things we ate, our breads and desserts were basic, assembled from the ingredients we could grow, gather, or carry across the water. But no one ever looked forward to fresh baked goods more than my sisters and I.

HAND-TOSSED FLUFFY BISCUITS

We always had some sort of bread in the house—with every meal and for snacks. If we had gravy with a meal, we had biscuits. And sometimes when we didn't have gravy, we had biscuits anyway.

Most days we worked right up to sunset. And as the sun fell low, Momma would be thinking about fixing supper. She would yell from across the yard to me: "Sallie Ann, go catch dat fire in da stove fo' me so dat oven can be hot by da time I get deh."

"Yes ma'am," I would answer, then drop my rake and hurry across the yard, because I knew she wanted that stove warm when she reached the kitchen. She didn't have to tell me she was making biscuits.

Quickly, I'd take off all three "lids" (or burners) on the stove, pack it with a pile of kindling and a couple larger pieces of wood, add a good pour of kerosene, replace all but one lid, and strike a match. Then I would make my arm as long as I could, turn my face away, and drop the match through the remaining hole in the stove top.

"Poof!" the stove would light, and I would jump back. As the fire started, I'd replace the last lid, and, like clockwork, Momma would walk through the door, telling me what to do.

"Gimme dat flour can," she'd say as she tied her apron, reached for the big bowl on the top shelf, and rushed about the kitchen. "Chile, git dem eggs out da bowl on da table, gimme da milk out da ice box, and han' me dat shortnin' off da shelf. Check dat fire, an' keep wood in da stove, an' keep it hot."

I knew someday I would be making my own biscuits, so I watched carefully. Momma made it look so easy as she made the dough and rolled it out on the table. But I knew it took practice. She'd reach for one of the jelly jars that we drank from, then let me press it down into the quarter-inch dough to cut out the biscuits. Next, she'd fill the bottom of a greased baking pan with the round pieces of dough, then hand it to me to place in the hot oven.

"Now don'tcha let dem biscuits burn or Ah'll have ya hide," she'd warn me, before turning to the rest of the meal. And even though I was ready to sneak a few more minutes outside, I stayed put.

2 cups sifted all-purpose flour
3 teaspoons baking powder
1 teaspoon salt
5 teaspoons cooking oil
¾ cup whole milk or buttermilk
2 medium eggs

Mix the dry ingredients together and fold in the oil. Slowly mix in the milk and eggs until combined. Sprinkle some flour on your table or counter or a large cutting board, knead the dough five or six times, and then roll it out to a thickness of ¼ inch or more (¼-inch-thick dough will rise to become a 1-inch-high biscuit). Bake in a preheated oven at 350° for 20 to 30 minutes, until golden brown, then brush on melted butter or margarine, if you like. Serve immediately, with butter, honey, jelly, syrup, or whatever you want.

GRANDMOMMA'S WOODSTOVE CORNBREAD

When Grandmomma was cooking, even before you took the first bite, you knew you wanted seconds. Baked, boiled, or fried, the food on her table was bound to be the best.

She was a big, bowlegged lady, who filled her homemade apron as she flowed across the kitchen, from water bucket to table to woodstove. As we played in the fenced yard or old field, the sweet 'roma would flow out, hinting at the wonders she was fixin' and mixin' inside. We weren't allowed in the kitchen, even to get a drink of water, because the water there was for cooking and she didn't want anyone in her way.

"Y'all chillen go play," Grandmomma would say. "Git from undah mah feet. Ya heah me!" And we'd be sure we did what she said, hoping she'd fix us her famous cornbread—which she would do two or three times each week.

It would rise up high above the pan, adding to any meal, from breakfast to a nighttime snack. We'd eat it on the side, or we'd pour syrup over it to make a full meal.

We may not live by bread alone, but with Grandmomma's cornbread, you could sho'nuff give it a try.

3 cups self-rising yellow cornmeal
3 tablespoons flour
2 eggs, beaten
1½ sticks margarine, melted
½ cup sugar
1–2 teaspoons vanilla extract
½–¾ cup clabber milk (curdled whole milk)

Pour the cornmeal and flour into a medium-to-large bowl. Then fold in the remaining ingredients. Mix well. Pour the batter into a greased 13 × 9-inch baking pan (it should fill the pan about halfway). Grandmomma placed the pan in the woodstove oven and propped a stick against the door to seal in the heat. You can place the pan in a preheated 350° oven and bake until golden brown (20 to 30 minutes).

BACON GREASE CORNBREAD STUFFING

2 cups water (divided)
8–10 chicken gizzards
½ teaspoon salt
½ teaspoon black pepper
4–6 strips smoked bacon
1 medium onion, diced
1 stalk celery, diced
1½ cups self-rising yellow cornmeal
2 tablespoons self-rising flour
2 hard-boiled eggs, chopped

Put 1½ cups water and the gizzards, salt, and pepper in a medium pot. Boil 45 to 60 minutes, until the gizzards are firm and a medium-thick gravy remains. Remove from the heat and set the gizzards and gravy aside to cool. Fry the bacon until crisp and then remove from the pan, leaving the grease. Add the onion and celery to the grease and fry a few minutes until the onion is clear. Crumble the bacon back into the vegetables and grease. Place the grease with bacon crumbs, onion, and celery in a mixing bowl; add the cornmeal, flour, and ½ cup water and combine thoroughly. Dice the cooled gizzards into fine (about ⅛-inch) pieces. Fold the diced gizzards, gravy, and chopped eggs into the cornmeal mixture, then mix well. Spoon into a greased 13 × 9-inch baking pan and bake in a preheated oven at 350° for 20 to 30 minutes, until the top browns and a straw or toothpick inserted in the stuffing comes out clean. Serve as a side dish or crumble and use to stuff a bird for roasting.

AGE-OL' CRACKLIN' BREAD

1½ cups white cornmeal
1 teaspoon baking powder
1 teaspoon baking soda
1 teaspoon salt
1 cup sifted all-purpose flour
1 cup whole milk or buttermilk
1 cup diced cracklin's (pork skin fried hard—available in many supermarkets)

Mix all the dry ingredients together. Add the milk and stir until smooth. Fold in the cracklin's. Pour into a hot, greased skillet or greased 13 × 9-inch baking pan. Bake 30 to 45 minutes in a preheated 350° oven until brown.

ROADSIDE BLUEBERRY BISCUITS

Just down the road from my grandmother's house grew a wonderful stand of wild blueberries. I guess the sunlight let in by the road clearing helped the bushes thrive. Since they were just outside Grandmomma's fence, where she could keep an eye on us from her kitchen window, she was happy to have us go picking there. And we were delighted when she turned our pickings into tasty biscuits.

½ teaspoon salt
½ cup sugar
2 teaspoons baking powder
2 cups all-purpose flour

½ stick margarine or butter
4–6 ounces blueberries, fresh or frozen
½ cup whole milk

Mix the salt, sugar, and baking powder together in a bowl. Add the flour and cut the butter (warmed to room temperature, not melted) into the mixture until it has the texture of coarse crumbs. Slowly fold in the blueberries and milk, stirring gently just to the point of combining. Form the batter into 1-inch balls and arrange on a greased cookie sheet or pan. Bake 6 to 8 minutes in a preheated oven at 350°, until golden brown. Serve hot or cold, as a side dish, snack, or dessert.

TREE-RIPENED APPLE PIE

Makes 2 pies

THE FILLING
10–12 crisp, fresh apples, peeled and sliced
½ cup water (divided)
2 cups sugar
2 teaspoons ground cinnamon
1 teaspoon ground allspice
grated peel (zest) of 1 lemon
1½ tablespoons cornstarch

Place the apples in a pot with about ¼ cup water, just enough to wet the bottom of the pot, since the apples have lots of water anyway. Add the sugar, cinnamon, allspice, and lemon peel (be sure to grate just the zest, or yellow skin). Boil 5 minutes. Mix the cornstarch with ¼ cup hot water, add to apples, and stir gently over low heat another 5 minutes or so. Don't overcook the apples to the point of mushiness.

THE CRUST

2 cups sifted self-rising flour
1 teaspoon salt
½ cup vegetable shortening (I use Crisco)
⅓ cup warm water

In a bowl, mix together the flour and salt, then add the shortening. Combine, using your hands, slowly adding the water as you mix, and then roll the dough out on a floured table, board, or piece of wax paper. Roll to about ⅛ inch thick, shape, cut, and place into 2 9-inch pie pans. Roll out cuttings and extra dough to make top crusts for the pies.

THE PIE

Scoop the filling into the pie shells, but fill only three-quarters of the way, so the filling won't bubble over the top when baked. Cover the filled pie shells with rolled out dough, pinching the edges between thumb and forefinger to seal the pies. Make a series of small slits in the center of the top crusts to allow steam to escape during cooking. Bake in a preheated oven at 350° for 20 to 30 minutes, until the crust is golden brown. Serve hot or cold, with or without ice cream.

TUMMY-YUM BREAD PUDDING

1½ loaves white or wheat bread (day-old bread works great)
¾ cup melted butter or margarine
1 cup sugar
3 eggs, beaten
1½ cups whole milk
2 tablespoons vanilla extract
½ teaspoon ground cinnamon
½ teaspoon ground nutmeg
16-ounce can fruit cocktail
8¼-ounce can crushed pineapple
½ cup chopped pecans
½ cup dark raisins

Tear each slice of bread into about 5 or 6 pieces and place in a large bowl. In a separate bowl, place the butter or margarine, sugar, eggs, milk, vanilla, and spices. Mix well, until the sugar dissolves. Add the fruit cocktail, pineapple, pecans, and raisins, and then gently fold in the torn bread, making sure it soaks up the liquid ingredients. Pour equal amounts of the mixture into 2 greased 13 × 9-inch baking pans. Bake in a preheated oven at 350° for 40 minutes, stirring once after 15 to 20 minutes. Stirring helps rich bread pudding bake evenly. Serve cold or hot, depending on the season and your mood.

Pinching the crust around the edges of an apple pie as fresh bread cools alongside.

STICKY-BUSH BLACKBERRY DUMPLING

I remember spring coming fast on Daufuskie. One day, it seemed, we'd be worrying about running out of firewood, and the next day the heat from the woodstove would be running us out of the kitchen. Pine pollen would turn everything yellow. The leaves would start falling from the live oaks. And everything would bloom—including blackberries.

Blackberry vines are hard to live around. Sharp thorns catch your clothing—and your skin, if you're not careful. Some vines would creep right into the grass, growing low, under the grazing cattle, and sticking us in our bare feet in the summer. Snakes love to hide out among the vines. And anywhere there's light, the blackberries grow and spread quickly. You can try to fight them back—and often lose—or you can live with them. We lived with them. They grew along most roads and in any field that hadn't been grazed for a few months.

Each spring, my sisters and I would watch impatiently as blackberry blossoms grew into green, then red, then purple berries. We'd test them as they darkened. And sometimes we tested too much and got sick. But we also knew that if we didn't pick the ripe berries quickly, the birds would beat us to them.

"Y'all watch where ya put ya foot fo' dem snakes," Momma would say when she knew we had berries on our minds. "An' don'tcha stain ya clothes."

We'd eat many more than we brought home. But even with our bellies full and our tongues stained dark, we—along with anyone else who had tasted our favorite dessert—couldn't wait for Momma to make dumplings.

THE DUMPLING

2 cups self-rising flour

½ cup sugar

2 tablespoons cooking oil
1/3 cup whole milk
2–3 cups fresh or frozen blackberries

By hand, combine the flour, sugar, oil, and milk into a dough and roll out into a 1/8-inch-thick circle on a floured counter or board. Set the dough atop a clean, dry cotton cloth. Wash and drain the blackberries, then place them in the middle of the dough. Lifting the edges of the cloth, wrap it and the dough up around the berries to make a ball, with the opening at the top. Seal the opening of the dumpling completely by pressing the dough together with your fingers, then tie the cloth together at the top to surround the dumpling. Place the wrapped dumpling in a large pot of boiling water and boil 20 to 30 minutes, until the dumpling is firm. Remove the cooked dumpling from the water and let it cool before unwrapping the cloth.

THE SAUCE
1/2 cup sugar
1 1/2 teaspoons vanilla extract
14-ounce can condensed milk
1/2 cup melted butter

While the dumpling cooks, mix together all of the sauce ingredients and simmer the mixture 8 to 10 minutes.

TO SERVE
Cut the cooked dumpling into individual portions and serve with a splash of warm sauce on each. Make more than you think you'll need, because you will eat it all.

SALLIE'S FAVORITE CARROT CAKE

1½ cups grated raw carrots (3–4 medium carrots)
1¾ cups all-purpose flour
1½ cups sugar
1 teaspoon baking powder
1 teaspoon baking soda
1 teaspoon salt
1 teaspoon ground cinnamon
¾ teaspoon ground cloves
¾ teaspoon ground nutmeg
¾ teaspoon ground allspice
1 cup golden raisins
1 cup walnut pieces
1½ tablespoons lemon juice
16-ounce can crushed pineapple, including juice
¾ cup vegetable oil
3 eggs, beaten
8 tablespoons softened butter
6–8 tablespoons pure honey

Mix all the dry ingredients in one bowl and all the wet ingredients in another. Combine the ingredients from both bowls and mix well. Pour the batter into 2 or 3 greased loaf pans and bake in a preheated oven at 350° for 40 to 50 minutes. The center cooks slowly, so test by inserting a sharp knife, a toothpick, or a broom straw, which should come out clean when the cake is done. The cake is rich enough to be served without icing, and may be served hot or cold.

THICK-CRUST PEACH COBBLER

10–12 ripe peaches, peeled and sliced
1 cup sugar
⅓ teaspoon ground cinnamon
¼ teaspoon ground nutmeg
½ cup melted butter or margarine
2 tablespoons cornstarch
7 tablespoons water (divided)
1½ cups all-purpose flour
½ teaspoon salt
½ cup vegetable shortening (such as Crisco)

Place the peaches in a medium saucepan. Add the sugar, spices, and butter (or margarine). Mix the cornstarch with 2 tablespoons cold water, then add to the peach mixture. Simmer, stirring gently, over low-to-medium heat, about 15 minutes, until a thick syrup forms. As the fruit cooks, place the flour, salt, shortening, and 5 tablespoons of warm water in a bowl and mix them together thoroughly by hand to make a dough. Pour the peach mixture into a greased 13 × 9-inch baking pan. Scoop tablespoons of dough into the peach mixture throughout the pan. These will cook and spread among the peaches as the cobbler bakes. Bake in a preheated oven at 350° for about 30 minutes, until the dough browns. Serve hot, with or without ice cream, as you prefer.

'FUSKIE PEAR BREAD

Blossoms on our three pear trees were among the first signs of spring. As the petals dropped, we'd count the tiny pears left behind to guess how much sweet fruit we'd have in August. We girls loved pears, and Momma's worst threats couldn't stop us from trying to eat them early.

"Doncha churn eat dem pears while we gone" would be the last words from her mouth as she and Pop headed off in the wagon behind our steer Bobby. No sooner had they cleared the end of the driveway than we would be out behind the house climbing the pear trees. We would eat the green pears until we were sick. Between our complaints and the pear cores lying in the yard, Momma always knew when we disobeyed her. A good spanking and a dose of her home remedy would follow.

One tree had hard pears, but the pears on the other two were softer, suitable for eating right off the tree—when they were ripe. On that day, Momma would call out to us girls, "Y'all go get dat bushel basket and start pickin' dem pears." After we had fought the bees, mosquitoes, and heat for the ripened fruit, she would line us up on the porch with bowls and knives. We would peel the pears and cut them into wedges—eating our share when Momma wasn't looking—then feed the scraps to the hogs and chickens. Momma made preserves from both the hard and soft pears, but separately, because they have different textures. They were all good, and any could form the base for pear bread.

This recipe, not really a "bread" in the usual sense, features pear preserves between two layers of crust. You can, if you like, subtract the dough ingredients and baking, add some sterilized jars, double or triple the recipe, and put up some pear preserves of your own.

This easy dessert was something Momma might make any day of the week if she was in the mood. And because she made it with preserves, we might have it any time of year. Sometimes we'd eat it hot, sometimes cold. Without refrigeration, it would keep fresh a day or two on the woodstove warmer. But the way we loved pear bread, a batch seldom lasted that long.

THE CRUST

3 cups sifted self-rising flour
1½ teaspoons salt
⅔ cup vegetable shortening (such as Crisco)
⅔ cup cold water

Prepare the crust first. Sift the flour and salt together. Add the shortening and combine by hand, then mix with cold water and roll the dough out about ⅛ inch thick on a floured table, board, or piece of wax paper. Cut the dough in two and press half into the bottom of a 13 × 9-inch baking pan, setting the other half aside for a top crust.

THE PRESERVES

15–25 small-to-medium ripe pears, peeled, cored, and cut into wedges
1½ cups sugar
½ cup water
1 teaspoon ground allspice
1 teaspoon ground nutmeg
1 teaspoon ground cinnamon
grated zest of half a lemon

Place the pear wedges in a medium pot over medium heat. Add the remaining ingredients and stir gently as the mixture warms, but don't let it come to a boil. Simmer 15 to 20 minutes, stirring occasionally. When the pears take on a reddish color, they're cooked.

THE BREAD

Allow the preserves to cool, then scoop them into the dough-lined pan. Add dough to form a top crust; drape it over the outer edge of the pan and seal it by pushing it against the pan with your fingers. Cut a few holes in the crust to allow steam to escape, and bake in a preheated 350° oven for 25 to 30 minutes, until the top crust is golden brown. Serve warm or cold and stand back, because the kids will be diggin' in.

SISTER'S POUND CAKE

½ cup melted butter
2 cups sugar
4 large eggs, beaten
2 cups sifted self-rising flour
2 teaspoons vanilla extract
1 tablespoon lemon juice

Combine the butter and sugar in a large mixing bowl. Using a hand mixer or standing mixer set on low, add the eggs, one at a time, to the sugar and butter. Slowly mix in the flour, then fold in the vanilla and lemon juice. Mix thoroughly. Grease and flour a loaf pan, pour in the batter, and bake in a preheated oven at 350° for 30 to 40 minutes. Test for doneness by poking the center of the cake with a toothpick, sharp knife, or broom straw; when the cake is done, the tester will come out clean. Serve alone or with fruit and/or ice cream.

PUMPKIN BREAD

2½ cups sugar
¾ cup cooking oil
4 eggs, beaten
3 cups self-rising flour
1 teaspoon ground nutmeg
1 teaspoon ground cinnamon
1 teaspoon salt
2 teaspoons baking soda
1 cup water
2 cups cooked fresh pumpkin or canned pumpkin
½ cup walnuts or pecans, chopped

With a whisk, mix the sugar, oil, and eggs in a bowl. Sift in the flour, spices, salt, and baking soda. Add the water, pumpkin, and nuts. Stir well. Pour the mixture into a greased 13 × 9-inch baking pan and bake at 350° in a preheated oven for 30 to 40 minutes. Test the center with a sharp knife, toothpick, or broom straw (which should come out clean) to be sure it's done. Serve hot or cold as a dessert or snack.

VINE-RIPENED PUMPKIN PIE

Makes 2 pies

THE FILLING

2 eggs
2 cups cooked fresh pumpkin or canned pumpkin
2 cups sugar

1½ teaspoons ground cinnamon
1½ teaspoons ground allspice
1½ teaspoons vanilla extract
1 cup evaporated milk
1½ sticks butter or margarine, melted

Beat the eggs in a large bowl, then add and thoroughly mix in all the other ingredients. The more you mix the filling, the smoother it will be.

THE CRUST

2 cups sifted self-rising flour
½ teaspoon salt
⅓ cup vegetable shortening (I use Crisco)
¼ cup warm water

In a bowl, mix the flour and salt together by hand, then add the shortening. Slowly add the water as you continue to mix by hand, and then roll the dough out on a floured table, board, or piece of wax paper. Roll to about ⅛ inch thick, shape, cut, and place into 2 9-inch pie pans. Pinch the dough around the edges of the pie pans to form scalloped crusts.

THE PIE

Pour the pumpkin mixture into the dough-lined pie pans. Bake in a preheated oven at 350° for 30 to 40 minutes, testing with a sharp knife, toothpick, or broom straw (which should come out clean) to make sure the filling is done. Serve warm or cold, alone or with ice cream.

SWEET TADA BREAD

6–8 medium sweet potatoes
2 sticks margarine or butter, melted
½ cup sugar
5-ounce can evaporated milk
3 large eggs, beaten
1 teaspoon vanilla extract
1 teaspoon ground cinnamon
1 teaspoon ground nutmeg
½ cup self-rising flour

Boil the sweet potatoes until soft (30 to 40 minutes). Drain and allow to cool. When cool, peel the potatoes and mash them in a bowl. In a separate bowl, mix together the margarine (or butter), sugar, milk, eggs, and vanilla. Add the cinnamon, nutmeg, and flour. Combine thoroughly with the mashed potatoes and pour into a well-greased 13×9-inch pan. Bake in a preheated oven at 350° for 30 to 45 minutes. Test with a sharp knife, toothpick, or broom straw inserted in the center of the bread; when the tester comes out clean, the bread is done.

SWEET TADA PONE

4 cups grated raw sweet potatoes (10–12 small-to-medium potatoes)
3 eggs, beaten
2 cups molasses or dark cane syrup
1 cup whole milk
¾ cup melted butter
1 cup sugar

1 cup self-rising flour
1 teaspoon ground cinnamon
1 teaspoon ground nutmeg
grated peel (zest) of 1 lemon
¼ cup dark raisins (optional)

Wash the sweet potatoes thoroughly, dry, and cut off the ends. Finely grate whole potatoes (use the same holes you would use to grate nutmeg) into a mixing bowl. Add the eggs and other liquid ingredients to the bowl and stir well. Continue stirring as you add the dry ingredients. Pour the mixture into a greased 13 × 9-inch baking pan. Bake in a preheated oven at 350° for 20 minutes. Remove from the oven and stir thoroughly. Return the pan to the oven and bake another 25 to 30 minutes, until a crust forms on top. Serve hot for a rich dessert.

 INDEX